PUBLIC RELATIONS
AND THE
SOCIAL WEB

PUBLIC RELATIONS
AND THE
SOCIAL WEB

How to use social media and
web 2.0 in communications

ROB BROWN

KOGAN PAGE

London and Philadelphia

First published in Great Britain and the United States in 2009 by Kogan Page Limited

120 Pentonville Road
London N1 9JN
United Kingdom
www.koganpage.com

525 South 4th Street, #241
Philadelphia PA 19147
USA

© Rob Brown, 2009

The right of Rob Brown to be identified as the author of this work has been asserted by him in accordance with the Copyright, Designs and Patents Act 1988.

ISBN 978 0 7494 5507 1

British Library Cataloguing-in-Publication Data

A CIP record for this book is available from the British Library.

Library of Congress Cataloging-in-Publication Data

Brown, Rob.
  Public relations and the social web : using social
media and Web 2.0 in communications / Rob Brown.
      p. cm.
  ISBN 978-0-7494-5507-1
  1. Public relations. 2. Internet in public relations. I. Title.
  HM1221.B765 2009
  659.20285'4678–dc22
                            2008049603

Typeset by JS Typesetting Ltd, Porthcawl, Mid Glamorgan
Printed and bound in India by Replika Press Pvt Ltd

Contents

	Preface	*ix*
1	**Something has happened to communications**	**1**
	The impact of a changing society	2
	How communications has changed	4
	The key milestones	8
2	**The implications for communicators**	**11**
	Fragmentation of the media	11
	Relinquishing control	14
3	**The lunatics have taken over the asylum**	**19**
	New routes to influence	21
	Conversations with the audience	23
4	**The new channels**	**25**
	Blogs	26
	Wikis	38
	RSS	42
	Podcasting	44
	Social bookmarking	48
	Social networking	50
5	**Digital PR and search engine optimization**	**53**
	How search engine optimization evolved	53

PR and natural search   55
Social search   57

6   **The power of the new media**   **59**
      The Scrabulous story   60

7   **The new ethics**   **67**
      The old ethics   68
      The new ethics and enlightened self-interest   72
      The wider impact   74

8   **The blurring of channels**   **77**
      Integration through disintegration   78
      It's the content not the channel   79

9   **The battle for influence at the digital frontier**   **83**
      The third wave of online influence   84
      Why the time has come for PR 2.0   85
      Issues management in the new Wild West   86

10   **Horses and courses**   **91**
      Evaluating the need for digital PR   92
      Politics   96
      Entertainment   102
      Industry and commerce   104

11   **Digital PR architecture**   **111**
      The same... but different   114
      Semantics   122

12   **Tools of the trade**   **125**
      The Social Media Release   125
      Social Media Newsroom   130
      Creative digital assets   131

13   **Evaluation and measurement**   **133**
      Search ranking as evaluation   135
      Online tools   136

Outsourcing 145
Things to consider 155

14 Dodging bear traps 157
Fact and fiction 157
We are in public 159
Brandjacking 159
Parody 160
Economies with the truth 161
Failing expectations 161
Tone of voice 162

15 The major players 163
Video sharing 164
Social networks 164
Photo sharing 169
Blogging platforms 170
Content sharing 172
Other communities 173

16 The next big thing 175
The rise (and fall and rise again?) of Facebook 175
Twitter – the early bird? 176
Born again Friendster 176
Huddle time 176
More mashups 177
Scour 177

Index 179

Preface

The impact of the internet on how we lead our lives has fascinated me since I first became aware of its existence. It dawned on me some years ago that we were all privileged to be living through one of the golden ages of communications; a period of major change. This book covers a small but significant part of that. When I started working in PR the world 'public' seemed to have very little to do with what we did, in fact the phrase 'media relations' more accurately represented the bulk of the activity carried out by public relations people. The radical changes that have taken place on the web have now brought PR people directly into contact with the public.

A couple of years after graduating, I worked for a new and forward thinking PR firm called Mason Williams who networked the PCs in the office. This meant that we could e-mail each other internally. I am not sure that we called it e-mail and the idea that you would be able to e-mail people anywhere was several years away but the possibilities were exciting and sometimes a little scary. Incidentally, the firm also had built into its word processor the first spell checker I'd ever seen. My colleagues and I all entered our names (or slight corruptions of them) and produced a set of instant nicknames; I was Rubble Brain. Very occasionally a former colleague will still call me Rubble.

A few years later when I was running my own business, I got my first internet browser on a disk from the front of a magazine and I was hooked. I could travel the world. I looked at a clock on the website of the University of Sydney, I was dumbstruck and started to consider the myriad of possibilities that the internet might afford. The Mosaic browser was the forerunner of Netscape Navigator which, although it was crushed by Microsoft's Internet Explorer, provided some of the code base for Mozilla Firefox. It is fascinating to see with the launch of Google Chrome that the browser wars continue to be fought and we face the possibility that the browser will become more important than the operating system.

I was invited to give lectures at Manchester Metropolitan University and the University of Central Lancashire on PR and the internet. In those days it was mainly speculation about what could happen but the impact started to be felt on the way we go about our business and it has continued ever since. Initially it was about how we did the same things in a different way, like sending photographs instead of send them. Now we are seeing altogether new ways of doing things and new things that we can do.

A few people asked me why I was writing a book about this subject rather than just blogging or publishing my own e-book. There are a number of reasons. One of the drawbacks of user generated content is the absence of an editor or a publisher. I felt if the book was to have any real value it should go through that process. In the book I discuss the concept of 'authority'. Books have an inherent authority, partly for the reason I have just mentioned, although some are more authoritative than others. There is another important reason. Just because a new form of communication comes along it doesn't mean that the old forms go away. We will always want to read books. We like their physicality and their tangibility. I do blog occasionally and you can follow me on Twitter. I won't tell you how to find these, if you don't know how to go about finding them you should do once you've read the book.

I have structured the book so that is has a kind of narrative and you will probably get the most from it if you start at the beginning and read through. There is also quite a bit of material that you can reference so if you'd rather dip in and out that should work too.

I never thought I would write a book about public relations, but then I never realized how much PR would change. This is a book about how radically public relations is changing. In a way this book is also about democracy as much as it is about PR. It is about the democratization of communications and how that in turn is bringing about the democratization of business and commerce.

1 Something has happened to communications

We are in the midst of a communications upheaval more significant than the introduction of the printing press. The change began in rarefied academic circles in the 1960s, gathered pace with the emergence of the world wide web in the 1990s, but exploded into its most decisive phase in 2004 with the arrival of Web 2.0. The term was coined by Dale Dougherty of the US publishing company O'Reilly Media and it was first used for the highly influential Web 2.0 conference run by the company in 2004. In reality, Web 2.0 had begun much earlier, but with the beginning of a new millennium, it gathered pace. The web has always been regarded as free but a new unregulated frontier was opening up in cyberspace. In the beginning, the 'coders' – computer programmers – had ruled the environment. Later, the graphic designers arrived and made their mark on the space. Now the web was finally opening up to anyone. Those with a spirit of adventure were staking claims to this virtual new territory.

Web 2.0 has a variety of definitions. It can be described simply as the version of the web that is open to ordinary users and where they can add their content. It refers to the sites and spaces on the internet where users can put words, pictures, sounds and video. It is a very simple idea in theory. In practice, it signifies the transfer of control of the internet, and ultimately the central platform for communication, from the few to the many. It is the democratization of the internet. The names of some of these spaces, Facebook, YouTube, MySpace and Wikipedia are now familiar. There are many thousands of others.

Nothing fundamentally changed in 2004 from a technological point of view; all of the tools that were available to create Web 2.0 environments already existed. What changed was the way that people started to view the internet. It was an organic change and it was driven as much by ordinary internet users as it was by large organizations. In fact, a number of those ordinary internet users created Web 2.0 environments that mushroomed into hugely valuable corporations and brands in a staggeringly short space of time. Bebo, the world's third-largest social networking website, was sold for £417 million to internet company AOL, just three years after being set up by husband and wife team Michael and Xochi Birch.

The impact of a changing society

The way that the internet has changed is a reflection of a much wider change in society. For a number of years leading politicians and social commentators have been talking about the 'end of deference'. In the Mackenzie-Stuart Lecture at the University of Cambridge Faculty of Law on 25 October 2007, Jack Straw, then Leader of the House of Commons said:

> There has been another major shift in society that is also relevant to this debate. The structure of British society, which developed during a century and more of industrialization, has rapidly been transformed as a result of changes brought about by economic globalization. This profound period of socio-economic change has helped to shift public attitudes. It has encouraged the rise of a less deferential, more consumerist public. In this more atomized society, people appear more inclined to think of themselves and one another as customers rather than citizens.

Historically, we were encouraged to believe that our best interests were served by accepting at face value what we were told by people in authority. The Central Office of Information for the Ministry of Health made a number of public information films in the middle of the last century that were so patronizing that they now appear to be spoofs. The following comes from the voice-over of a film entitled *Don't Spread Germs*:

> Now, let's get this quite clear; you sneeze into the handkerchief, and then put the handkerchief into the bowl of disinfectant to kill the germs not in with the family's washing. Got it? Sure? Good! Remember: Don't spread Germs.

If you want to see the clip and others like it, they are available online in the National Archives at http://www.nationalarchives.gov.uk/films/1945to1951/filmindex.htm.

The tone is extraordinary and quite different from modern public health messaging. The UK government's current campaign to get people to use tissues rather than handkerchiefs is all about advice and persuasion — offering people packs of tissues in exchange for handkerchiefs. Another modern case in point is the government's quit smoking campaign. The film is almost all about fellow smokers who have decided to give up. It is all about empathy and shared experience with the minimum use of an authoritative voice.

Web 2.0 is both a reflection of these changes and a major instrument for the acceleration of this shift. Consumers have the ability to talk back and to share their views and opinions with other consumers. They no longer implicitly trust what they are being told and this has major implications for the ways that brands communicate. Historically, organizations would decide on the image that they wanted and on how they wanted their various audiences to view them and then it would fall to the PR advisors to make that happen. What has happened is that the organizations have lost control of the agenda. In order to influence how they are seen they have to participate in conversations. Whilst for some this might appear to be a frightening change it is highly beneficial for the consumer and ultimately for the enlightened organization as it will draw it much closer to the people who use its products and services.

Independently of the changes that are happening in digital environments, we have seen the emergence of organizations and businesses that have a more democratic and inclusive culture than those that preceded them. One of these is innocent, the fruit smoothie-maker and the epitome of a modern brand. Its packaging actually invites people to call the office or even pay a visit.

How communications has changed

Communications is undergoing a radical change. Every aspect of how we exchange information is feeling the impact of the technological revolution. Changes are taking place in the way we use the media channels that have been available to us for many years. Totally new communications channels are emerging. The PR practitioners of the 21st century must understand all of these and how they are controlled and influenced if they are going to adapt and survive in this new environment.

Newspapers and magazines

Newspapers and magazines gave PR practitioners their first taste of the evolving media landscape. The early web versions of offline titles were essentially mirrors of the printed versions but they started to create opportunities for extended PR coverage as they rolled out revised websites that contained content that was unique to the web. As they started to refresh content more frequently, something significant changed for PR. The web news pages effectively killed off the concept of the embargo. The structured announcement of PR stories to ensure that a key monthly title could carry a PR story on the same day as a daily paper came to an end when news organizations could release stories literally within minutes of receiving them.

Major newspapers are in the business of reinventing themselves as brands. Their future role will be to disseminate news across a variety of platforms. When the *Guardian* relaunched itself in the smaller Berliner format in 2005, the editor, Alan Rusbridger, said at the time that the *Guardian* website was cannibalizing newspaper readership and that this was a factor in the prior fall in the paper's circulation. He also said something else that provided a fascinating insight into the future of national daily newspapers. The new format required the purchase of new printers at some considerable cost: £62 million, £12 million more than the paper had budgeted. The editor apparently said that he thought they would be the last printers that the paper bought. Given that the lifespan of these presses could be as little as 20 years, this suggests that for some national papers the future will not involve paper at all. In fact, if you want to keep up to date with modern media trends, one of the best places to garner information on new trends is part of the new age *Guardian*. Media Talk is the Guardian Unlimited media podcast hosted weekly by Matt Wells and available via iTunes.

Television

There are a number of significant changes happening to the way we watch television. One of these is viewer scheduling. Innovations like Sky+, BBC iPlayer and TV content on iTunes mean that we can watch favoured programmes when it suits us and not just when they are broadcast. Incidentally, it also means that we can choose to skip TV adverts. The iPlayer and a number of similar platforms also mean that we are not just watching TV on the box in the corner of the living room but we are watching it on PCs, laptops and mobile devices, including iPods. Major manufacturers have cottoned onto this and have developed attractive-looking compact PCs that come with remote controls and are designed to operate through your TV. In 2008, Philips launched the EasyLife LX2000 computer with no monitor, designed to be attached to your TV like a DVD recorder and optimized for TV and video content viewing.

The natural conclusion is that content from broadcasters and from other sources including those that incorporate user-generated content (UGC) will start to converge. Moving from BBC iPlayer to Sky to stored content on your PC or streaming content from the internet will all be done in the same way that we used to channel hop. This means two things for the PR practitioner. The first is that there are more direct routes to market for TV or video. The second and related point is that the content needs to be genuinely engaging. In this new environment, content is king of kings and viewers will watch what they want and not just what they are fed.

There is another interesting issue that anyone involved in content production should consider. Big TV screens in the living room will become ubiquitous, the quality is improving with better high definition and the costs are falling. At the same time, TV is starting to appear on iPods and mobile phones. These two concurrent developments create a dilemma. Will something that works on a 52-inch screen also work on a 2-inch? Not always.

Finally, as the TV and the computer finally converge, the opportunities for integrating the functionality of Web 2.0 and the engaging nature of good TV should prove exciting for communicators in every field.

Radio

Due to the greater simplicity of radio and the lower 'bandwidth' requirements, radio has been available across a range of platforms for some time. Radio downloads that aren't ever broadcast in a traditional sense are becoming increasingly popular. We just don't call it radio; we refer to them as podcasts. In fact, the Director of the Radio Academy, Trevor Dann, is in no doubt that radio and podcasts are essentially the same thing:

> The Sony Radio Academy Awards has a special category for the internet radio programme and I think it's important that it's called an internet radio programme and not a podcast or audiostream because we shouldn't define the content by the form of delivery. (Trevor Dann speaking on BBC Radio Five, 24 March 2008)

Podcasts are incredibly cheap and easy to produce and simple to make available. The key, however, is content once again. It is an easy mistake to assume that because it is a low-technology environment anyone can do it. As PR people we should continue to value the skills of people who have developed their art and technique in the highly competitive broadcast environment to help us create podcasts that our audiences will choose and want to listen to.

The internet

Is the internet a medium at all? I really don't think that it is – it is far richer and more complex than any of the traditional media channels. At one level it provides a platform that to varying degrees allows the traditional channels to migrate their content and reach different audiences. On another level it delivers a series of new media platforms and has created the forum through which the consumer and the brand can interact. For example, Facebook, as the leading social networking site, has characteristics all of its own. In fact, it doesn't even regard itself as a social networking or social media site; it describes itself as a social utility. It is also a perfect example of how platforms on the internet mesh and mash up with each other. For example, YouTube provides a great deal of content for Facebook. Essentially, the way Facebook works is to draw content and applications from the widest possible range of sources. We will explore these internet-based platforms in more detail later in the book.

Whilst this book concerns itself with the growth and evolution of new digital channels it is important not to approach these channels in isolation. I believe that the distinction between digital and offline will gradually disappear. The distinctions will become blurred, as we are starting to see with radio and television, and the number of platforms will grow. For example, the growth of hand-held mobile channels will create new opportunities as we integrate location and content. Knowing where our audience physically are at any one moment will have a dramatic influence on what we want to say to them.

The other important consideration is that traditional media will not go away. In that regard I am entirely persuaded by the view of Gary Carter, President of Creative Networks at FremantleMedia and Chief Creative Officer, FremantleMedia New Platforms. In a keynote speech at the National Association of Television Program Executives conference in Las Vegas in January 2007 he argued the following:

The simple historical fact is that mass communication technologies are never replaced by newer technologies. They coexist, while continuing to evolve. We still have the newspaper, the telephone, the radio, and the movies, despite the fact that each of these was at the time of introduction viewed as the beginning of the end for the other.

The only mass communication medium in history to have been replaced by another is the telegraph, a service which began in 1851 with the founding of the New York and Mississippi Valley Printing Telegraph Company and spanned 150 years, ending finally on 27 January 2006 when Western Union discontinued the service. Western Union report that telegrams sent had fallen to 20,000 per year, due to competition from other communication technologies, including — and probably mainly — e-mail. Arguably, of course, the telegram was not a mass communication technology.

The key milestones

The key milestones in the development of Web 2.0 from its beginnings until the time of writing are as follows:

- 1969
  - Generally recognized as the year the internet was born or indeed the ARPANET as it was called after the Advanced Research Projects Agency Network responsible for its beginnings. The first computer in the network was at UCLA (Los Angeles), closely followed by nodes at Stanford Research Institute, UCSB (Santa Barbara) and the University of Utah.
- 1973
  - The first international connections were made to the ARPANET at the University College of London and the Royal Radar Establishment in Norway.
- 1979
  - News groups were created with the arrival of Usenet, a collection of discussion groups. This signalled the arrival of

user-generated content a quarter of a century before the Web 2.0 concept came into being.

- 1991
  - The world wide web came into being, having been developed by Tim Berners-Lee to provide easy access to any form of information anywhere in the world. This was closely followed by the launch of Mosaic, the first graphic web browser.
- 1997
  - Jorn Barger, who runs a site called Robot Wisdom, coined the term 'weblogs' to describe the phenomenon, then in its very early days, which we have come to know in the shortened form 'blogs'.
- 1999
  - RSS (Really Simple Syndication) feeds were first introduced – the basis for allowing people to receive blogs and podcasts. Blogger, the simple-to-use system for creating and uploading blogs also comes into being.
- 2001
  - Wikipedia, the online encyclopaedia that can be edited by anyone, was launched by Jimmy Wales and Larry Sanger initially as a feeder providing an additional source of draft articles and ideas to the expert-written project 'Nupedia'. It quickly eclipsed Nupedia.
- 2003
  - MySpace was founded allowing users to build networks of friends and incorporate personal profiles, blogs, groups, photos, music and videos.
- 2004
  - Caterina Fake and programmer Stewart Butterfield created Flickr, the photo-sharing site that they later sold to Yahoo!. It became one of the web's fastest-growing properties. Caterina and Stewart were a husband and wife team like Bebo founders Michael and Xochi Birch.
  - Facebook launched initially for founder Mark Zuckerberg's fellow students at Harvard University.
  - In the same year US publishing company O'Reilly Media coined the term Web 2.0 at the seminal Web 2.0 conference.

- Two months later Digg launched. Digg is a site that allows users to discover and share content from anywhere on the web — users collectively determine the value of content and it is ranked accordingly, thereafter impacting traffic across the web.
- 2005
  - YouTube, the video-sharing website where users can upload, view and share video clips, was created in mid-February 2005 by three former PayPal employees, Steve Chen, Chad Hurley and Jawed Karim.
- 2006
  - Twitter was launched as a free social networking and micro-blogging service that allows users to send 'updates' of up to 140 characters to the Twitter website.
  - Google Inc. announced that it had reached a deal to acquire YouTube for US$1.65 billion.
  - Facebook became open to the general public.
- 2007
  - Microsoft Office 2007 was launched with the ability to create blogs 'built-in' to the software.
- 2008
  - Bebo is sold by its founders to AOL.
  - Candidates in the US presidential race use Facebook and YouTube as an integral part of their campaigns.

2 The implications for communicators

The radical changes in the communications infrastructure have a range of implications for the public relations and other marketing communications industries. Our task is more difficult because there is greater complexity, however there are considerable advantages. There are new routes and channels through which messages will flow and this significantly enhances our ability to target the audiences that we are interested in. The old-style definition of public relations talked about organizations communicating with their 'publics': a series of large groups of people identified by something that they all shared in common. Perhaps they lived or worked in the geographical area surrounding a particular factory. They might share broad interests. Now we can target groups on a much narrower basis.

Fragmentation of the media

In less than 30 years, the United Kingdom has gone from having three television channels to having more than 300. With the arrival of Internet Protocol Television (IPTV) it is quite conceivable that we could have more than 3000 'channels' within a short space of time – although the concept of a TV channel is beginning to be eroded. In the same period of time we have seen an explosion in the number of radio licences and the arrival of Digital Audio Broadcasting (DAB) and numerous internet radio stations. The web has also given us access to radio stations from all over the world.

The growth in the number of channels has also seen a greater diversity of content. Broadcasters are targeting narrowly defined groups of people identified by interests, their social demographics or their culture. For years we have had bridal magazines; now we have Wedding TV. There are channels devoted to individual sports like racing and golf and those devoted to niche programming genres like The Biography Channel.

In the days before multi-channel television there were few opportunities for PR people to engage with their audience through the mass television medium. Now there are many and varied opportunities but television has ceased to be a mass medium.

Increasing choice always means declining numbers

The most watched US television programme of all time was the last ever episode of the black comedy series *M*A*S*H*, set in a mobile army surgery in South Korea. It was broadcast on 28 February 1983. In fact, nine of the top 10 programmes of all time were broadcast in a 10-year period between 1976 and 1986. The only exception was the women's figure skating event in the 1994 Winter Olympics featuring Nancy Kerrigan and Tonya Harding. Sporting events still draw large crowds but this particular event had a special significance, which explains why it drew such a large audience some eight years after the end of the golden age of high-rating shows.

Tonya Harding had been implicated in a physical attack on her rival Nancy Kerrigan and the news of her alleged involvement created a media frenzy. CBS assigned its star reporter Connie Chung to follow Harding's every move during the Winter Olympic Games in Lillehammer, and Harding was featured on the cover of both *Time* and *Newsweek* magazines in January 1994. The ratings-busting showdown was in February. An interesting side note to this is the fact that the world wide web was effectively still in its very first year of existence; the Mosaic web browser that effectively opened the web to all had only been released in April of the previous year.

For many years in the United Kingdom the leading executives at ITV and the BBC searched in vain for programmes that would restore the Saturday night TV audience to the scale of those of the late 20th century. They hunted for the successors to 'Brucie' and 'Tarbey' (Bruce Forsyth and Jimmy Tarbuck), TV presenters who would deliver audiences of in excess of 10 million week in week out. In recent years presenters Ant and Dec have come closest to the national icons that in former years guaranteed gargantuan advertising revenues for Saturday night slots on commercial television.

The big audience numbers have gone and viewing figures have continued their steady decline. Today's TV presenters are a match for their predecessors and it is not the case that the programmes are any less engaging. It is simply the fact that the audience has found other places to go, other programmes to watch, other times to watch them and other media to consume.

A further trend that media watchers have detected is that Saturday night in front of the box in the corner of the living room has ceased to be a family event. A large part of the explanation is that TV viewing amongst the young is declining at a faster rate than it is for the population as a whole. Those born in the era of the web will never have the same attitude to television as the preceding generation. If they want to watch something in a passive way they will do it on their own terms, often downloading or streaming the programming to personal PCs so that they can watch exactly what they want, when they want to. On Saturday nights they may be watching TV, but if so it is unlikely to be something that has been scheduled for them. Alternatively, they are highly likely to be consuming or, rather, participating in another medium. The social web is a place or a series of virtual places where these people are engaging with others like them: sharing content rather than simply consuming it, talking, swapping ideas and interests, recommending things for their friends to watch or read and consuming a variety of media on the recommendations of their peers.

Relinquishing control

If the content that people are engaged with is content that they are contributing to, if the media that they are consuming allows them to participate, it becomes very clear that the rules of engagement have changed. If the owners of the means of communication no longer control the content, and essentially that is the substance of Web 2.0, then the principles of marketing must fundamentally change. The movement away from deference and from top–down communications is embodied in the new architecture of digital media.

The *Guardian* newspaper has been one of the prime movers in taking and adapting its product online. One of the most important developments has been made on the realization that news is now no longer the preserve of journalists. In the majority of cases there will always be individuals closer to the action than a journalist and the *Guardian* has made it possible for those individuals to add comment and have it viewed alongside the work of more conventional journalists. With the 'commentisfree...' element of the site the newspaper also permits anyone to add their individual views and opinions. Whilst the *Guardian* does retain editorial control over this content, the nature of that control is markedly different from the way a newspaper edits. The most significant difference is that any edits or deletions are made after the articles or comments are posted, rather than before. By the middle of 2008 the *Guardian* was receiving up to 10,000 postings a day to its site – far too large a number to moderate before they appear. It was always a point of contention amongst journalists if editors interfered with their copy, but it was always understood that that was their prerogative and an aspect of their role (unless you are journalist and broadcaster Giles Coren, whose expletive-ridden letter on the subject to his subeditors was widely distributed on the web). In digital news environments the conventions are quite different. Postings are regarded generally as sacrosanct. They may be deleted altogether if they are deemed to be illegal or, for example, if they promote hatred, but they are very rarely edited. This ceding of control exhibited by major news organizations clearly means that PR people need to extend their contacts beyond those with conventional journalists.

The rules for brands have also changed. The arrival of the internet gave organizations an opportunity to engage more actively with their stakeholder audiences. The use of websites allowed businesses to provide new information in new ways and to ensure that the information was up to date. The first wave of corporate websites were, however, little more than electronic brochures. The most successful corporate websites now have to engage their users. If you look at the travel sector for example, an operator that sees the internet as merely an extension of the holiday brochure with beautiful pictures, flowery copy and no opportunity for consumers to add their experiences in an honest and open way is probably doomed to ever-dwindling site traffic with all that represents for bookings. Any operator in the sector will also be aware that sites like TripAdvisor play a really important part in the holiday booking process for many travellers

The breaking of brand rules

This creeping loss of control is having an impact on how we perceive brands and how brand identities can be managed. The growth in the power of brands was in part achieved by the strength of the visual imagery associated with them. If we could rewind to the beginning of the 20th century we might regard it as unthinkable that a very sugary, dark-brown-coloured drink might become one of the most powerful brands of that century. Coca-Cola, in fact, created many of the brand rules using visual cues. First, there is a very simple but distinctive colour palette. The drink was packaged in an iconic and immediately identifiable bottle. Then there was the logo, a memorable name in a script so distinctive that you didn't need to read it to know what it was. There were the brand guardians, the employees of Coca-Cola whose job it was to ensure that no element of the brand was copied or displayed in a way that fell foul of the brand guidelines. Woe betide anyone who, as I once did in my early days as a PR account handler, drafted copy in which the two halves of the word Coca-Cola were split across two lines.

Brand guidelines with their accompanying brand books have become a familiar part of the armoury of large organizations. At the very core are the rules on the use of the brand logo. The precise colour references, the colours of background on which it may be used, how it is to be displayed in monotone, how far from a border it may be printed, are all ubiquitous parts of the instruction manuals that are given to designers and others permitted to use the logo.

A very interesting 'craze' has arisen in recent years. People began to analyse how brands in the digital world were mimicking the brand rules of the past and the new devices that they were using to appear modern and distinctive. For example, the use of the word 'Beta' in the logo as a way of both demonstrating how new a site was but also getting the excuse in early if anything did not work entirely as planned. Unusual names emerged or a common word might be corrupted by, say, dropping a vowel, as in 'Flickr'.

Not only were people unconnected with the organizations analysing logos but the design programs needed to create and adapt logos have quickly become universally available. Not surprising then that people invented their own spurious logos. From there it is a short leap to the craze for reinterpreting the logos for iconic brands as if they were new web brands. Package delivery company UPS has built a well-chronicled narrative around the use of a particular shade of brown for its logo and all of its livery. It polices the utilization of the colour with great vigour. If you look for a Logo 2.0 interpretation on the internet you should be able to find a new-look UPS logo in a rather vibrant, perhaps even lurid green. My personal favourite reinterpretation is the one for 'QUAKR 2.Oats'.

This craze is in many ways completely harmless fun. What is interesting is the ease with which anyone can go to the heart of what brands spend fortunes trying to protect and overturn all of the rules.

Fear of the recalcitrant

Brands have woken up to what is happening and it is creating concern in the boardroom. The Web 2.0 world feels like the Wild West to them. There are people staking claims to territory, there are outlaws and there are wild rumours of huge fortunes to be made. This is a digital frontier where the laws of the old world do not apply and a place where the intractable, wayward and headstrong can raise their voices against the might of the old corporations. There are some already celebrated examples of major brands and corporations capitulating in the face of online challenges. There have been some true David and Goliath battles and the giants of the business world are starting to understand that they cannot control the conversations about their brands, products or businesses in the way that they used to.

Dell hell

The true power of the blog was first properly established with a cause célèbre that became known as 'Dell hell'. Jeff Jarvis is an American journalist and a former television critic for *People* magazine. He was also associate publisher of the *New York Daily News* and a *San Francisco Examiner* columnist. In the United Kingdom he has a column in the *MediaGuardian* supplement.

Jeff has his own blog called BuzzMachine, which became the focus of his negative experiences in dealing with his new Dell computer and the company's customer support in 2005. Jeff wrote a blog post with the title, 'Dell lies. Dell sucks'. He has subsequently said that all he wanted to do was warn off other unsuspecting customers by adding just one more critical consumer opinion to those already on the web. His post, however, generated an astonishing level of resonance with other dissatisfied Dell users. Readers left comments with their Dell hell experiences and other bloggers linked to the post with their tales of woe. The blog continued with the saga of unhappy experiences: home service that he couldn't get, replaced parts that didn't work and e-mails that went unanswered. At first he was ignored but as interest gathered pace he was contacted by Dell and it replaced his machine.

That wasn't the end of the saga. The blog resulted in press coverage from newspapers, magazines and other blogs and was credited with a significant decline in Dell's customer satisfaction rating, market share and share price.

To some extent the story of Jeff Jarvis and Dell continues and the impact of his blog on the fortunes of the computer giant goes on. In October 2007 Jeff wrote the lead article in the influential title *BusinessWeek*, for which he conducted an interview with Michael Dell. The company has been reported to have spent over $150,000,000 on customer service since the postings began.

Because of this, many businesses are fearful of Web 2.0. They are starting to realize that the PR profession has a new role to play but they feel very uncomfortable about participating in an environment where the consumer talks back.

The choice

Ultimately, the choice for organizations is a simple one: they either take part in these conversations or they don't. What they have to realize though is that if they don't participate in these conversations they won't simply go away. The dialogue will go on without them. This means that for businesses of the future the choice isn't simple at all. There is no choice. Brands will have to participate in dialogue in order to survive. The consumer demands it and we should all embrace it. It will make brands better. More heads are better than one.

Brian Solis, the leading PR 2.0 evangelist and exponent, sums it up in his contribution to *The Social Web Analytics eBook 2008* by Philip Sheldrake of Racepoint:

Social Media is no longer an option or debatable. It is critically important to all businesses, without prejudice. It represents a powerful, and additional, channel to first listen to customers, stakeholders, media, bloggers, peers, and other influencers, and in turn, build two-way paths of conversations to them. Yes, conversations are taking place about your company, product, and service, right now, with or without you. This represents priceless opportunities to build relationships and shape perceptions at every step. In the process, you become a resource to the very people looking for leadership, expertise, vision and solutions. The most important driver for outbound and proactive online relations is that it's measurable and absolutely tied to the bottom line.

3 The lunatics have taken over the asylum

If the old brand guardians are no longer in control and the media is becoming disparate and fragmented, who should public relations people be talking to? The answer, ultimately, is quite simple and the clue is in the description 'public relations'. PR people need to be talking to the public just like they have always done.

In the context of broader marketing communications, these changes herald a new era in which the targeting skills of the public relations industry are infinitely more adaptable and appropriate to the environment than those of the traditionally more dominant advertising industry. The techniques of above-the-line communications have evolved to suit the process of mass communications in the broadcasting era. Advertising ideas are usually distilled down to a single powerful idea. Audience targeting requires a focus on a very narrowly and carefully defined conceptual target. It is not at all uncommon for large organizations advertising a mass-market product to attempt to define the audience that they are trying to reach by defining a single archetypal individual who is the embodiment of that audience.

Public relations has always talked about target audiences as a plurality of publics; different groups of people with different ideas, interests and levels of involvement with whom we would converse in different ways. It is easy to see why the PR approach to defining audiences is well suited to this fragmented environment.

For the media old guard it might seem as if the lunatics have taken over the asylum but in reality this is just another chapter in the long-running battle for control of the message. The British Labour politician, Tony Benn, attacked the BBC in a speech in 1968 that foreshadowed some of the changes that we are seeing now but also referred to the fact that this is a part of a continuing and ancient struggle for influence:

> Broadcasting is really too important to be left to the broadcasters, and somehow we must find a new way of using radio and television to allow us to talk to each other. We've got to fight all over again the same battles that we fought centuries ago to get rid of the licence to print and the same battles to establish representative broadcasting in place of the benevolent paternalism by the constitutional monarchs who reside in the palatial Broadcasting House.

Nearly 40 years later George Osborne, a politician of quite a different political hue, acknowledged in a speech at St Bride's church in Central London, that the populous was now in control:

> With all these profound changes — the Googleization of the world's information, the creation of online social networks bigger than whole populations, the ability of new technology to harness the wisdom of crowds and the rise of user-generated content — we are seeing the democratization of the means of production, distribution and exchange... People are no longer prepared to sit and be spoon-fed.

They are taking matters into their own hands through their blogs and online networks and user-generated content. They are organizing political campaigns and building coalitions based around common interests. They are spreading news and information to one another on a scale never before thought possible. They are the masters now.

New routes to influence

In the corporate as well as in the political world, we are starting to see a whole host of new routes and opportunities through which we can communicate with our audience. In many ways the old problem of how to influence the journalists who control the means of communication is being eclipsed by a completely new problem. There is a plethora of routes and channels that are open to us but discovering which channels carry the most influence and authority is the real challenge now.

The increasingly tangled web

In recent years, Google has measured the extraordinary exponential growth in the sheer scale of the internet. In order to be able to search the internet Google must first be able to index it and this is a process that involves continuous updates. The first Google index to be announced in 1998 estimated that the internet already had 26 million pages. It only took two years for the Google index to reach the 1 billion mark. In recent years, we've seen a lot of big numbers about how much content is really out there. The official Google blog announced in July 2008 that its own search engineers stopped in awe when they discovered that their systems that process links on the web to find new content hit a new milestone: 1 trillion (or in digits 1,000,000,000,000) unique pages. The number of individual web pages is still growing by several billion pages per day.

One aspect of the rapid growth of user-generated content and the recognition of the importance of this content being linked to lots of other related content is that the web is becoming increasingly crowded, congested and complicated. The explosion in the range and volume of content is matched by an inverse relationship with the average level of importance and impact of a single web page.

Seeing the wood for the trees

Given that we are operating in a complex environment it is critical that we are able to differentiate the parts of the internet that are important to us and that have influence from those that are simply backwaters or blind alleys. We have a very simple tool available to us in the form of 'search', which for most of us still means Google. The front-page rankings on any Google search give us a pretty good idea where the web traffic is heading for that particular topic.

Search on its own is a fairly blunt instrument. The PR practitioner needs to know more about what is going on in relation to their brand or client. This is not simply about numbers or the number of hits that particular websites or communities get. In judging where web content is important and has influence we need to get to grips with the concept of 'authority'. Broadly, the concept of authority on the web is the same as the concept of authority elsewhere but on the web it can be measured. A very good example of this is via Technorati, one of the most widely recognized ways of measuring what is happening on the web, particularly with what it calls 'citizen media'.

Technorati.com includes the Technorati Authority numbers for blogs. Technorati Authority is the number of blogs linking to a site in the previous six months; the bigger the number, the greater the authority. The Technorati Top 100 lists the blogs with the most authority. If you create content that is interesting to other bloggers then they are more likely to link to your site or blog, thereby increasing your authority. Creating these links is also a way of engaging in conversation with other people who may have influence and authority. You can actually show your Technorati Authority on your blog or web page with the Technorati Authority widget available from the website.

There are lots of other guides to influential blogs; for example, the AdAge Power 150 lists the most influential media and marketing blogs. There are actually nearer 1,000 ranked on this list rather than the 150 suggested by the title. The list also uses Technorati Authority as one of several factors in computing the order of influence of the inclusions.

Conversations with the audience

PR people are used to thinking about consumers as an audience. We now have to think about a significant proportion of that audience in a different way. They are no longer passive but active participants in a conversation. This does not only mean that we should converse with them but it also means that we have to give their views and opinions due respect. We must always remember that these conversations are held in public and will remain in the public domain for the foreseeable future and in some cases perhaps forever.

How, where and when

The 'how' about these conversations is the same as the 'how' about any conversation. Say something interesting and start a debate. It is a subtle but fundamental difference to the old approach. If you are just making pronouncements, you are saying something that you find interesting or important. You imagine and hope there will be a willing audience out there somewhere. For a conversation to take place you need to give the particular interests of your audience more consideration. The days have gone where we issue a story that the client insists upon, knowing that a trade title or two will print it in return for a 'colour separation' fee and knowing that no one will read it, but at least there will be something for the cuttings book. To be successful we must engage and we need to advocate the importance of that to our clients and colleagues.

The 'where' is a little more complicated. There are a variety of places where you can start a conversation. One of these is the corporate website, which should be enabled with forums or comment sections. Increasingly, corporate bodies are blogging and this is a far better place in which to start a conversation. I will cover some of the pros and cons of a corporate website in the next chapter. Blogs are of their very essence conversational; if a web post doesn't have a comments section it isn't really a blog. Corporate blogs are less 'top–down' and autocratic in their style than corporate websites. For example, the profile section of a corporate website would feature the job titles and perhaps a short career history of senior executives.

Where the same people are profiled in a corporate blog it is much more likely to refer to their personal interests and may not mention their job title at all. Forums are perhaps an even better place to engage. They are the traditional locations for conversations on the internet and they provide an even playing field. We should also be engaging conversations on the blogs of individuals and other relevant organizations.

The 'when' is now. My only caveat to that is that before you engage in a conversation, you should read the posts and comments that have already been made and become accustomed to their conventions. The discussions are taking place already and you should not hesitate too long before joining them.

4 The new channels

Whenever we hear that the internet is the fastest-growing medium, as we often do, I become somewhat vexed. I really don't believe that the internet is a medium in the way that radio, television and newspapers are media. The internet is a network that is able to carry and support most of the other media. We perhaps compare the internet to television because we traditionally access it through a box with a screen in the corner of the room. However, the devices that we use to access the internet are becoming many and varied, from mobile phones and other hand-held devices to products that use the internet for a very specific purpose. An example would be music centres obtaining information about the MP3 tracks that they are playing. The internet is a delivery mechanism that is fast becoming the preferred route through which we access television, radio and much of our newspaper content as well as many, many other things. For want of a better word I think we can use the idea of 'channels' to group some of those other things together. Even within these new channels we discover huge levels of complexity. If we take, for example, social networking we might start with Facebook. Within Facebook there is a plethora of applications and ways of drawing in content from other Web 2.0 applications.

Blogs

The word is a contraction of 'weblog'. It is difficult to say exactly when blogging started. Jorn Barger, editor of the blog Robot Wisdom, effectively invented the term weblog to describe the process of 'logging the web' as he surfed. Barger remains a peripheral figure with some questionable political views. His blogs continue but his low authority (see Chapter 3) probably only rates at all because of his role in coining the term in December 1997. The term 'blog' was not used for another two-and-a-half years. It was first employed by Peter Merholz, who, when he first used it, intended it to be a joke. He broke the word weblog into two words 'we blog' in his own peterme.com blog. In doing so he essentially created the verb 'to blog', meaning to create a weblog as well as initiating the contraction of the noun into its now popular form.

The first bloggers were the effectively online diarists, who would keep a running account of their lives. These blogs began well before the term was coined and the authors referred to themselves usually as diarists or online journalists. Perhaps the first of these and therefore the original blogger was Justin Hall, who began blogging in 1994 and posted his first regular blog 'Justin's Links from the Underground' whilst still a student.

Blogging took off when the publishing platform Blogger was launched in August 1999. It quickly became the most popular and simple to use blogging tool and it allowed mainstream internet users with little or no technical knowledge to start blogs. Blogger was bought by Google in 2003.

The cultural and political significance of blogs was imprinted on the collective consciousness when the second Iraq war broke out and with the arrival of the 'Baghdad Blogger'. A blog from inside Iraq called 'Where is Raed?' appeared, authored under the pseudonym Salam Pax. The blog discusses the war, Salam's friends, disappearances of people under Saddam Hussein and the impact of the military offensive from inside Iraq. Many people wondered whether it was real or if it was a sophisticated piece of propaganda. The site's name refers to Raed Jarrar, a friend of Salam's (which turned out to be his real given name) who was studying for a master's degree in Jordan.

Because Salam couldn't reach Raed by e-mail he set up the blog for him to read. In May 2003, the *Guardian* confirmed the widely debated question that Salam was a real person who was living in Iraq, and added that he was 29 years old and an architect. The site was temporarily blocked by the Iraqi authorities but for most of the war, he gave accounts of bombings in Baghdad until the electricity went down and Pax remained offline for weeks. In August 2004, several months after he had posted on 'Where is Raed?' Pax started a new blog entitled 'shut up you fat whiner!'. He later briefly worked as a journalist for the *Guardian*.

For those of us that wish to engage with bloggers we need to bear in mind that the explosion in the sheer number of blogs means that most of them will seldom, if ever, be read. At the time of writing, Technorati was tracking 112.8 million blogs and over 250 million pieces of tagged social media and typing the word 'blog' into Google produced over 3.2 billion results.

What is a blog?

In many ways a blog is similar to a website but a blog is generally held to have some defining characteristics. Blogs have a title, they usually have a date stamp and they almost always allow comments to be attached. Blogs are usually maintained by an individual although this is not always the case. Where a blog is maintained by an organization or a corporate body it is almost always made clear who the individuals are within that organization who are responsible for the blog and it is often made clear that their opinions are personal rather than the views of the corporate body. Entries are typically regular or at least frequent, sometimes daily, although again this is not always the case. These entries are usually listed in reverse chronological order. Many blogs cover a particular subject; others are more like personal online diaries. For PR persons it is the blogs that cover specific subjects that are of the most interest to us.

Blogger engagement

One of the terms that is bandied around in digital PR circles is the phrase 'blogger engagement'. There are a number of ways that this can be done. First, I'd like to go a little deeper into the nature of what a blog actually is and what a blogger actually does.

Many blogs are engaged in a form of participatory journalism, but they tend to differentiate themselves from mainstream journalism. Many bloggers are in fact journalists who are simply operating in a different environment. Some journalists see the blog as a way of getting their views and opinions directly to the audience without any editorial interference.

There has been much debate in PR circles as to whether bloggers are the new journalists. Personally, I think it is interesting that many of the people who say blogging is not journalism are the same people that have disdain for the term PR 2.0 and regard digital PR as being exactly the same as old-style public relations. How can that be so? In a way I think they are wrong on both counts. There are thousands upon thousands of bloggers and most have little relevance or influence. For many of these people it is simply about the pleasure and excitement of being able to self-publish. For those that operate at the apex of the pyramid I believe that the similarity between what they do and what a good journalist does bears a great deal of scrutiny.

In terms of engagement it is widely agreed that bloggers dislike getting press releases; well, so do most journalists that I have met. I firmly believe that we can engage with these bloggers in the way that we do with our journalist contacts — by e-mail and by telephone and on the odd occasion by actually meeting.

So if we can deal with some bloggers in the way that we deal with the press then that suggests, doesn't it, that this new form of public relations is just the same as the old? Well, some bits of it are and some aspects are entirely new. It has also made the world considerably more complex and requires us to develop a wider range of skills and knowledge. The traditional skills of the PR person are particularly useful in this new environment where much of the media has become socialized. In addition to talking to bloggers offline we can have a conversation with them very simply online just by adding a post or a comment to their blog. Remember that this is a conversation in public and that mostly they will talk back.

A concept that is widely discussed by those interested in the digital arena is that of 'The Long Tail'. The phrase 'The Long Tail' was used by Editor-in-Chief Chris Anderson in an October 2004 *Wired* magazine article and it is also the title of his blog. He used it to describe the strategy of certain types of business, particularly those that have had success online where, in addition to items being sold in large quantities, there is a long tail of products sold in increasingly small numbers to ever-diminishing groups of customers.

The concept of a frequency distribution with a long tail has been around for a very long time. Before the internet, the media industry made its decisions based on the notion of a normal distribution of customers – targeting the largest audience sectors found at the peak sector of the bell curve. Now internet-based media adopt a long tail strategy with increasingly tailored output for increasingly narrow audiences.

A famous posting by Chris Anderson in his 'Long Tail' blog offers a very salutary lesson for PR people who approach bloggers with the old-fashioned scattergun press release approach. The posting was logged on 27 October 2007 and entitled 'Sorry PR People: You're Blocked'. In the posting Chris refers to the fact that he gets over 300 e-mails a day from PR people. He says they are untargeted and inappropriate and equates them with spam. He also goes further: he names the PR people, he lists their e-mail addresses and informs all of them that they are blocked, permanently. This is a pretty severe censure for a PR person as it also prevents them from making a targeted e-mail approach to Chris at any time in the future unless, as he suggests, they use a different e-mail address. There were 329 e-mail addresses on the list that he published and they included some names from very eminent PR companies including the world's largest, Weber Shandwick and Edelman, widely regarded as the global trailblazer in digital public relations.

What we need to understand as PR practitioners is that if Chris Anderson is doing this and writing about it then other journalists and bloggers are doing this without our knowledge. This means that the concept of the press release is in an inevitable decline. Because we now send out press releases by e-mail it is possible for journalists to block the person and not just the press release. In the days of paper press releases the most common response to receiving a press release was to spike it. This originally meant quite literally pushing the piece of paper onto a spike on the journalist's desk. The change in the dynamic is quite interesting here. By spiking a press release rather than immediately binning it, there was at least the theoretical option that it could be retrieved and used later. By deleting and blocking, the journalist or blogger is ensuring that not only does the press release never ever get used but also that the PR person sending it can never approach them in this way again.

The social web provides us with tools for engaging with bloggers that were unavailable to us in our dealings with journalists. A good example of how we can do this is by using a micro-blog like Twitter to pitch our story. I will explain the 'twitpitch' later in the chapter.

Perhaps things aren't quite as different as this makes them seem. For years PR people have found better tools to use than the blunt instrument of the press release. Journalists have always objected to receiving poorly targeted press releases. I suspect that for many, once they had received three or four badly aimed missives from a particular individual or organization, that was the point at which they spiked everything that they ever sent.

How to blog

Far and away the easiest way to get started is to use an online blogging platform, and it is very easy is to use a blogging platform like Blogger or WordPress. Both of these services are free to use, and you can get started on your blog very easily, with a minimum of set-up.

Using Blogger as an example, simply follow these simple steps. Go to www.blogger.com and click on the 'Create Your Blog Now' banner. Use any e-mail address that you have to create a Google account: this will take about a minute, then click on the continue arrow at the bottom of the page. Fill in a title for the blog and create a web address in the box below. Verify a random word that has been generated on the screen – this is simply to demonstrate that you're a human being and not a web-bot – and click on the continue arrow. You are then invited to select a template for your blog. There are quite a number to choose from and they will determine the look and feel of your blog when it is published. That is it. Well not quite, you have to start adding content. There is a text editor into which you can start typing and you can add photographs by clicking on the icon in the text editor. It is simple and quite possible for you to have a blog online within five minutes of going to the Blogger website.

The ease with which we can blog means that a key element is often forgotten – that of quality. One of the most important things that distinguishes a blog from other forms of written published content is the absence of an editor or a publisher to select, moderate or adapt the content. There is no quality threshold that the blog has to pass through in order to be published. We can publish anything we like; there is no arbiter of taste, decency or quality. The function of publishers and editors in ensuring quality content is ultimately to drive popularity in terms of circulation and readership. Without their moderation, bloggers are solely and entirely responsible for the quality of their output. The one measure that remains is that of popularity and readership. If it isn't good very few will read it, none of them will come back and they will recommend it to no one. Never underestimate this. User-generated content has accelerated the growth of the internet, which passed the milestone of 1 trillion unique pages at some point during the middle of 2008. With so much out there most of it is going to be ignored. It is essential that there is an interested audience for what you are publishing and the content had better be good.

Make sure you get the basics right as well. There will be no separate proofreader and no grammar checker. If you aren't good at these things get someone to check your posts before you publish. A blog with spelling mistakes or poor grammar will be the kiss of death, even if the quality of the writing is good.

The importance of the quality of writing is not new and there is an excellent short guide to writing written in the 1950s by Paul McHenry Roberts. Roberts taught English for over 20 years, first at San José State College and later at Cornell University. He also wrote a number of books on linguistics, including *Understanding Grammar* (1954), *Patterns of English* (1956), and *Understanding English* (1958). The guide is called 'How to Say Nothing in Five Hundred Words' and if you want to read it in full it is available at http://www3.baylor.edu/~Jesse_Airaudi/nothingwords.html. It is worth a read, and 500 words is a pretty good length for the average blog.

One of Roberts' core arguments is that it is our job to make every subject engaging. As he says in the guide:

Can you be expected to make a dull subject interesting? As a matter of fact, this is precisely what you are expected to do. This is the writer's essential task. All subjects, except sex, are dull until somebody makes them interesting. The writer's job is to find the argument, the approach, the angle, the wording that will take the reader with him.

This argument is as valid now as it was half a century ago. Roberts also makes a series of powerful arguments:

Avoid obvious content

When arguing a case take an original position. It is better to be original with a less defensible position than to trot out a well-argued but hackneyed point of view.

Take the less usual side

Debates are intellectual exercises; take a position that looks hard and is the least defensible. It will make it easier to write something interesting.

Slip out of abstraction

If you want your reader to believe you, you must take them with you. Examine the work of professional writers and notice how they constantly move from general abstract statements to concrete examples.

Get rid of padding

The statement 'In my humble opinion, though I do not claim to be an expert on this complicated subject, fast driving, in most circumstances, would seem to be rather dangerous in many respects, or at least so it would seem to me' can be shortened to 'fast driving is dangerous' (example from Roberts, 'How to Say Nothing in Five Hundred Words'). Forty words have been reduced to four without losing any content at all. If you want to add content then do it by adding meaning. Roberts continues:

You illustrate. You say that fast driving is dangerous, and then you prove it. How long does it take to stop a car at forty and at eighty? How far can you see at night? What happens when a tire blows? What happens in a head-on collision at fifty miles an hour?

Call a fool a fool

Decide what you want to articulate and say it in plain words, make your case vigorously and do so without apology or prevarication. Avoid the temptation of calling a spade 'a certain garden implement'. Roberts again:

> Writing in the modern world, you cannot altogether avoid modern jargon… you can do much if you will mount guard against those roundabout phrases, those echoing polysyllables that tend to slip into your writing to rob it of its crispness and force.

Beware of pat expressions

As Roberts says, in the same essay: 'Other things being equal, avoid phrases like "other things being equal."'

Colourful, coloured and colourless words

Roberts again:

> The writer builds with words, and no builder uses a raw material more slippery and elusive and treacherous. A writer's work is a constant struggle to get the right word in the right place, to find that particular word that will convey his meaning exactly, that will persuade the reader or soothe him or startle or amuse him.

Should corporates blog?

The early blogs were followed by a rush to corporate blogging but the question still remains as to whether the personal nature of the average blog translates well to a corporate environment. With Google and other search engines favouring sites that are regularly updated, blogs are very likely to boost a company's presence in search rankings in a way that a traditional corporate website will not, and therefore the idea of a corporate blog can be very compelling.

Businesses can be nervous about the naked conversations that take place in and around blogs and there have been cases where careless comments have hit a corporate share price. The greater danger is that a corporate blog will be entirely anodyne, with no company insight or genuine thought leadership. There is an argument that says that corporate blogs should only be written by the chief executive because any other author is likely to play safe and avoid any kind of controversy. Vetting of blogs, reliance on press releases and overcaution are all likely to result in a blog that nobody actually wants to read.

Blogs should also allow comments. In the case of most corporate blogs, as with many personal blogs, the comments are moderated. Businesses tend to block any challenging comments or any that generate real debate and this also tends to result in something that is dull and uninteresting. As Bob Pearson, Vice President of Corporate Group Communications at Dell says:

> A lot of companies are making the mistake that blogging is publishing… Blogging is two-way and, crucially, it's the audience that decides what's read, what gets linked to and so what is deemed successful. So it makes sense to listen to the conversations your target consumers are having and then shape your blog around them.

So should corporates blog? The answer to this is a qualified yes they should, but they need to be careful and need to do it properly. Blogs that are promotional or simply use copy cut and pasted from press releases will be passed over and will have no impact. We have to ask the questions, is the blog going to be interesting and is it going to be relevant to its target audience? Once you've started the blog you will quickly discover whether the answer to these questions is yes.

There are also some critical things to avoid. You should never ever be tempted to run a seemingly independent blog in favour of a client by pretending to be someone unconnected with the organization.

Apart from being unethical, this practice, along with the practice of posting comments and contributing to forums whilst cloaking your identity or not declaring an interest is often referred to as 'astroturfing' (or creating fake grassroots opinion), it is likely that you will be found out. This will create significant damage for your brand or organization. It goes without saying that you should also avoid the more extreme version of this, known as 'sock puppetry', the practice of posting entries under several different false names to make something look more popular than it is.

In 2005, part of the L'Oreal cosmetics empire produced a fake blog called 'Journal de ma Peau', to promote an anti-wrinkle product called Peel Microabrasion. It was the testimony of a woman called Claire, who had great experiences with the product and claimed that it improved her skin. Claire, despite her claimed advancing years, looked like a professionally photographed model and one with precious few wrinkles. Claire had been invented by an advertising agency. The company received so many complaints in just two months it was forced to replace the fictional Claire with real-life bloggers who described their genuine experiences.

Fake blogs have been ruled as an unfair commercial practice by Brussels. Firms breaking the rules may face prosecution, stiff fines and possibly even jail terms for its staff. The European Union's Directive on Unfair Business-to-Consumer Commercial Practices, makes these online deceptions illegal. Companies and/or employees can be held liable, with fines starting at £5,000 but with no upper limit and prison sentences of up to two years, which can be imposed in the most serious cases.

There are some significant risks associated with blogging, partly because of the absence of filters that apply to most forms of publication. This is an issue for a corporate body and companies should place their own filters and controls to minimize the risks from corporate blogs. Take the example of Simon Uwins, a UK marketing director for Tesco who went to the United States to take the marketing director role for Tesco's US 'Fresh & Easy' chain. He posted the following on his company's corporate blog:

Wednesday, March 26, 2008
Pausing for Breath at Fresh & Easy

Phew! We've opened 31 stores in 66 days so far this year... now we're pausing for breath. We've been delighted with the openings. There's always been a line of customers waiting for each store to open. Indeed at some, such as Long Beach pictured above, the lines were almost too long, they took hours to clear – I'm sorry if anyone was inconvenienced.

And every week, we attract more customers in our existing stores. However, after opening our first 50, we planned to have a 3 month break from openings, and other than a couple more in Phoenix, we're taking it (albeit, in our usual fashion, with 59 stores already open).

Why? Quite simply, to allow the business we've created to settle down. In 9 months, we've gone from a project team of 200 people to a business employing nearly 2500 people – and in another 9 months, it'll be over 5000. In a little over 4 months, we've gone from a business with no stores to one with 59 – with hundreds more in the pipeline. We've learnt a huge amount about running the operation, and talked to thousands of customers about what they like about Fresh & Easy, and where they'd like us to improve. So we've given ourselves a little bit of time to kick the tires, smooth out any wrinkles, and make some improvements that customers have asked for.

This appears to be quite innocuous stuff, very open and honest, customer-orientated and very much in line with the way corporate should be behaving in a Web 2.0 world. However, Simon Uwins had told the market something that they did not know, which combined with the hint that the store opening programme might not be going as successfully as planned suggested a problem. When the news contained in the blog circulated, Tesco's shares dropped 11.25p to 379p, wiping not far short of a billion pounds off the value of the company (albeit temporarily) and market traders attributed this to the blog.

Micro-blogging

Micro-blogging is a form of blogging that allows users to write extremely short text-only blogs. They are usually restricted to a maximum of 140 characters. Users can then choose to publish them so that anyone can read them or restrict them to a group. The character limit means that these messages can be uploaded by a variety of means, most significantly via SMS texts, which means that they can be uploaded anywhere and any time. The most popular micro-blogging service is Twitter, launched in July 2006, and users of Facebook will be familiar with a micro-blog on their Facebook page known as their 'Status'.

Although micro-blogging is similar to blogging, the nature of it means that the way it is used is quite different from the way that longer blogs are used. Twitter users attending recent technology conferences have started tweeting, or sending Twitter micro-blogs to speakers from their seats in the audience in the middle of their presentations. For PR people promoting any kind of event or programme where the audience or stakeholders require or would be interested in short, regular updates, Twitter can offer a new dimension to their communications programme.

Barack Obama started using Twitter in April 2007 as part of his campaign to be president of the United States. Although generating relatively small numbers of followers compared with other forms of communication, he acquired nearly 40,000 followers to his micro-blog within a year. It would be reasonable to assume that this 40,000 included people of influence and authority in disproportionate numbers. For example, one imagines that a political journalist following the US presidential election would probably subscribe to Obama's Twitter feeds. Obama used these short messages not only to make his campaign more personal but also to provide neat sound bites describing political views and opinions. British Prime Minister Gordon Brown has also used Twitter but somewhat less successfully. Perhaps the fact that he was not involved in a campaign means that micro-blogging was a less relevant communications method. His Twitter account was also spoofed. The spoof version included the following 'tweet' posted in the days shortly before he took over the reins from Tony Blair: 'havent signed tonys card yet, can't think of anything funny to put'. It was subsequently changed to a Downing Street twitter rather than something that was personal to the prime minister and as a result works less well. The spoofing of the account also demonstrates the very many pitfalls that anyone operating in this totally open environment might encounter.

As I intimated earlier in the chapter, Twitter provides us with an interesting new way to pitch ideas to bloggers. The so-called 'twitpitch' is an elevator pitch condensed further to just the 140 characters allowed by Twitter. The idea was conceived by Stowe Boyd of the \Message blog who says: 'Basically, I want companies to get their story down to a one-liner "escalator" pitch – like 10 seconds long – which is going to force them to drop the superlatives and buzzwords and get to the heart of the matter.' It works by including something called a hashtag, which can be achieved simply by prefixing a word with the hash key. In this example the hashtag would simply be the word #twitpitch, which would be contained in the tweet. The twitpitch could be an invitation to an event, meeting (a 'tweatup'... oh dear) or a telephone conversation, the inclusion of a single URL, or a 130-character written pitch. A feature of twitpitches is that they are open – anyone can search on the hashtag. Boyd explained:

> I want these PR types to do their business in the open, so that others can see their pitches. It's good for them and their clients if the pitches are short and sweet, suggest a real value to someone, and avoid buzzwords and fuzzy analogies. My 'followers' on Twitter can get the benefits of a discourse about these products, if there is any benefit to be had. And it's all done in the clear light of Twitter.

Wikis

The first site to use the term 'wiki' was WikiWikiWeb created by Howard G. 'Ward' Cunningham, a US computer programmer in 1994. He gave it that name because a Honolulu International Airport counter employee told him to take the 'Wiki Wiki' or quick shuttle bus that runs between the airport's terminals. Cunningham said thereafter that he 'chose wiki-wiki as an alliterative substitute for "quick" and thereby avoided naming this stuff quick-web'.

A wiki has come to be understood as a series of web pages designed to enable anyone who accesses the site to add content or modify the content that is already there. It works because wikis use a simplified markup language and therefore can be altered by individuals without a technical understanding of HTML (HyperText Markup Language). By far the best-known wiki is the collaborative encyclopaedia Wikipedia.

Wikipedia was launched on 15 January 2001, and was founded by Jimmy Wales and Larry Sanger. Within a year it had acquired 20,000 articles, and appeared in 18 languages. As of December 2007, UK Wikipedia had over 2 million articles, making it the largest encyclopaedia in history.

Almost every article in Wikipedia can be edited anonymously. Registered users can create new articles. There is a 'History' page attached to each article containing all of the previous versions of the article (libellous content, criminal threats or copyright infringements are removed). The content is constantly changing and although it is not peer reviewed in the same way that traditional encyclopaedias are it is effectively reviewed by anyone with an interest.

In an interview on 26 August 2006 with Trevor Jonas of Bite PR, co-founder of Wikipedia, Jimmy Wales, intimated that PR people should not edit Wikipedia or wikis in general. He said:

> I think that PR firms editing in a community space is deeply unethical, and that clients should put very firm pressure on their PR firms to not embarrass them in this way... It is a bad idea because of the conflict of interest. It is perfectly fine to talk to the community, to show them more information, to give them things that show your client in the best light. But it is wrong to try to directly participate in the process when you have an agenda... Ironically, the ones I directly deal with are the ethical ones, the ones who approach me and ask how to do things. I tell them: post to the discussion pages, talk to the community. The problematic ones are the ones who try unethical things like editing behind a fake ID.

Jimmy Wales presents us with a very difficult challenge. I think that the problem we have is the differentiation he makes between ethical

PR firms and individuals, and what he regards as the mainstream PR industry. It is our challenge to persuade people like Jimmy that ethics are at the heart of the mainstream.

From a philosophical point of view it is generally agreed that there is no such thing as total objectivity. Therefore, Wikipedia and other wikis are in fact the product of a series of subjective opinions and interpretations.

We have a number of options. The first is to refrain entirely from adding information to or editing any content on any wiki. I believe that this is clearly draconian and impacts on one of the central aspects of what we do, which is to act as a channel of communication placing information and knowledge into the public domain. We, whilst refraining from adding content to wikis, could advise our clients or in-house colleagues as to how they go about adding content. However, I believe for organizations to provide content about themselves is a clear conflict of interest as defined by Wikipedia.

We should at this point consider one of the key roles that strategic public relations advisers have always performed. We have always provided strategic counsel on what an organization should say about itself and a central tenet is that this information should be truthful. We are therefore better placed to be objective about an organization we represent than the organization itself. It is quite ludicrous to suggest that all public relations people are unable to write from a neutral point of view.

For the best advice on how people with vested interests can and should contribute to wikis, I have turned to Wikipedia itself. First, start by declaring your interest. Wikipedia does not give advice about how to do this but it encourages you to do so. Your interest may be partially self-evident from an e-mail address but you may also want to state your interest on Wikipedia's talk pages (more of these later). In declaring an interest at the earliest outset you ensure that other Wikipedians are less likely to question your good faith. Your input may attract additional interest and attention and encourage more edits by others, but we should see this as a good thing rather than a bad one. This kind of disclosure invites help from others. You must be neutral but if there is inaccurate bias against your company and its interests, there is no reason why you should not seek to correct this. Unsupported defamatory content can be removed immediately and Wikipedia specifies that anyone can and should do this. This is an occasion where the PR person's interest coincides with that of Wikipedia and articles that attack or are inherently hostile can be nominated for immediate deletion and will be removed. There will inevitably be grey areas. In these cases it is probably best, as Wikipedia suggests, to discuss corrections on the associated talk page.

Near the top of a Wikipedia article you will see a tab marked 'Discussion'. Click on this and read the guidelines as to how to edit and add content to the discussion. You will have to identify yourself either through your IP address or by registering. You are also expected to sign your posts. Using the talk page can often be a precursor to corrections or additions to the main article. You should make it clear why you are using the talk page and declare any conflicts of interest.

There are some cases where it is reasonable for PR people to edit the main article. For example, removing spam or perhaps correcting mistakes you yourself have made. In addition you can upload digital media files, such as audio files, video clips and photographs to Wikimedia Commons – in fact, interested parties are encouraged to do so and conflicts of interest are not an issue here. When these media files are sent to Wikimedia Commons, they are often used in the relevant Wikipedia articles. Once again you can use the article's talk page to make Wikipedians aware that the images or clips are available. If an image is clearly relevant and you have the rights to use it then it can be added directly to the article.

There is probably no occasion when an organization or its PR advisers should properly author an entirely new article. It is totally acceptable though to suggest that a new article should be created. This can be done either through a Wikiproject (a collection of articles devoted to the same broad topic) or by adding the suggestion to the talk page of a similar or related article.

Finally, we must remember that wikis are self-regulating and self-correcting, which means not only that promotional copy has no place here but also that it will be deleted or amended quickly and as a matter of course. Wikipedia calls this the law of unintended consequences:

Wikipedia's Law of Unintended Consequences
If you write in Wikipedia about yourself, your group, your company, or your pet idea, once the article is created, you have no right to control its content, and no right to delete it outside our normal channels. Content is not deleted just because somebody doesn't like it. Any editor may add material to or remove material from the article within the terms of our content policies. If there is anything publicly available on a topic that you would not want included in an article, it will probably find its way there eventually. More than one user has created an article only to find himself presented in a poor light long-term by other editors. If you engage in an edit war in an attempt to obtain a version of your liking you may have your editing access removed, perhaps permanently.

In addition, if your article is found not to be worthy of inclusion in the first place, it will be deleted, as per our deletion policies. Therefore, don't create promotional or other articles lightly, especially on subjects you care about. (http://en.wikipedia. org/wiki/Wikipedia:Ownership_of_articles)

RSS

RSS will soon become one of the principal pillars of any PR campaign or programme. I will explain what an RSS feed is and how it works. RSS stands for Really Simple Syndication. It didn't always stand for that; in fact it first stood for RDF (Resource Description Framework) Site Summary, but frankly that's something of a red herring here. RSS is a web feed format used to publish content. Web content like blogs, news headlines and podcasts can be published in a standard way using RSS. This makes it possible for users to keep up to date with a whole series of sources of information without having to check back to the sites that they are interested in. An RSS aggregator can show content from multiple web sources in one place. The user subscribes to the RSS feed by entering a link into their reader or by clicking an RSS icon that automates the process. The RSS reader checks the original sources regularly and downloads the updates.

This all sounds a bit techie so I will try to describe it in a different way. Let's start with the RSS aggregator. This is just one of many programs or sites that allow you to use RSS. Internet Explorer, Firefox and Safari do it, Microsoft Outlook does it, Google and Yahoo! do it and there are a host of other programs and web-based applications that can handle RSS feeds. Think of an RSS reader as being like a news ticker or just a list of news headlines in a box on your screen. You can click on the headlines and the program will show you more content or take you to the original sources. Even if you are unfamiliar with the concept of RSS, I'm pretty sure that you will have already seen an RSS reader somewhere without knowing what it was called — it is just a list of news headlines.

For these headlines to appear in an RSS reader, the original content has to be RSS-enabled. This means creating a web feed for your site. A web feed is a document written in XML (Extensible Markup Language). You make this document available on your site and users can copy and paste into the software that reads RSS feeds. Depending on the program, you might subscribe to a feed by manually entering the URL of a feed or clicking a link in a browser. This process is becoming more automated and user-friendly all the time.

Having explained what it is and how it works I think I should explain why I think RSS is so important for PR people. Let's go back to the example shown by Chris Anderson of *Wired* magazine. Given that the press release is in decline and can so easily be blocked we need to find another way of talking to multiple journalists and other interested parties that is as speedy and efficient as issuing press releases but that is better targeted. How would it be if we could ensure that every single press release that we send out went to somebody whom we could virtually guarantee would be interested in its content? In a sense that's what RSS can do for us. By posting press releases that are RSS-enabled, those people that get them are people that have chosen to receive them. There is, as always, a difficulty. What if nobody chooses to take the RSS feed? Well, in essence we are facing the same problem that PR people have always faced if they send out dull press releases – nobody will be interested. You will have heard the phrase 'content is king'. We now operate in an environment where everyone can publish and everyone can choose what they read, view or listen to. In this environment, ensuring that all of our content is engaging has become critical.

There are some real challenges to using RSS. For example, we might choose to create a restricted press room in which to place our feeds, so that the consumer does not have the same immediate access to our news as does the journalist, which would obviate any reason for the journalist to use our copy. In other circumstances and in campaigns we might want to use RSS as a way of directly reaching interested stakeholders or consumers.

By combining RSS feeds with micro-blogging you can create a very effective tool for disseminating information and links in an automated fashion that will not only potentially reach an influential audience but also send them directly to your main blog posts. You can 'tweet' your headlines by using an application called Twitterfeed to push your blog's RSS feeds directly to Twitter. It effectively gives your blog a route for 'breaking news' and news that is 'new' is always more popular.

Podcasting

When I talked about podcasts in Chapter 1, I drew some very clear parallels with radio. The principal difference is the delivery system. Whilst the radio is broadcast, podcasts are actually syndicated in almost exactly the same way as RSS feeds. The term 'podcast' is a fusion of 'iPod' and 'broadcast'. Although many podcasts can be downloaded directly from the publisher, broadcaster or originator's website, a podcast is essentially defined by the fact that it is syndicated, subscribed to and downloaded automatically using RSS 2.0. This book is not intended to be highly technical nor is it my particular area of expertise but the RSS 2.0 evolution of RSS is important because it allows enclosures to be included, for example MP3 files, and this is what made podcasting possible.

The programs or sites that are used to aggregate and download podcasts are different from those that aggregate the RSS text feeds. The most familiar of these is iTunes. There are many others: Juice, Podget and FeedDemon are examples. Although the way they work varies slightly, subscribing to and listening to podcasts is very easy. You click on the title of the series of podcasts that you are interested in; every time a new episode is syndicated the program downloads it and sends it to your MP3 player whenever you dock your MP3 player with the computer.

Podcasts can be listened to on any type of MP3 player or on a computer. The types of devices that can play MP3s are becoming more numerous. For example, many in-car GPS navigation systems can play MP3s and send the audio via an inbuilt FM transmitter, making it easy to listen to podcasts on your car radio.

As the audiences for particular podcasts grow they become of greater interest as channels and the PR community will start to target them in a similar way to traditional radio. Podcasts are and will be more receptive to receiving finished audio than radio programmes have been, particularly if the content is interesting and it is directly relevant to the content of the podcast. These could be submitted as MP3 files and e-mailed to the podcast producer.

Podcasting as a means of syndicating audio material can be used in a variety of ways that go beyond the remit of radio. For example, they can be used as an educational tool and one of the biggest uses and growth of podcasting is in teaching foreign languages. Podcasting is a valuable way of delivering information about events, conferences or festivals. Podcasts can be used as a way of involving people who are unable to attend by making available recordings of events and interviews or other feature material.

Creating podcasts

'User-generated content' (UGC) is at the heart of everything that is changing on the web and PR is about promoting and generating content. The content, however, that we are best at generating is written information. If we go back in time, PR people weren't just producing press releases, we were writing copy for newsletters, brochures and reports. We were sometimes also called on to write scripts for corporate videos. Producing audio or video is not a core skill of the public relations professional so we have to be cautious about how we decide to generate this content. Simply producing audio is not that difficult but there are people for whom this is a core skill and we should consider every case on its merits and decide whether something is best created in-house or better subcontracted to a specialist in the field.

If you do decide to make the podcast, here are a few tips. You need a basic studio that will consist of a microphone and recorder. You can choose to use a stand-alone digital recorder or record direct to PC. The latter is preferable because it means the finished audio file will be where you want it to be when you are ready to publish it. There are now MP3 players on the market that allow you to record as well as play back. These are excellent if you need to be mobile but you will still need to edit your files on a digital recording device.

If you are going to record to PC you need the means to convert the analogue audio signal that comes from the microphone to a digital signal that can be recorded on your computer and you need recording software. The analogue to digital conversion is done using an audio interface or sound card. These have become quite cheap – Behringer, M-Audio and TASCAM are some of the names to look out for.

In terms of the software, there are some very good solutions that are available to download free. Audacity is available from audacity. sourceforge.net. It will allow you to record live audio using multiple channels at once (up to 16). It will import audio for you to edit and then save in a variety of formats including WAV and MP3, which is the format that you will need for uploading your podcast. It includes a variety of audio effects and allows you to clean up your recordings, remove hiss, hums and other background noises.

There are other more sophisticated programs designed primarily for music recording that offer a huge range of recording and audio engineering capabilities. The names that you could look out for include Cakewalk, GarageBand (for Mac users) and Samplitude. Your final podcast should be saved as an MP3 file and should ideally be 5 MB to 50 MB in size.

I have barely scratched the surface of podcast production here and there is a lot more that you will need to teach yourself. It's not overwhelmingly difficult but unless you have a real desire and interest I would recommend that you get in a professional.

Publishing your podcast

We know where to get our podcasts – from aggregators like iTunes or Juice, but how do they get there in the first place and more importantly how do we put them there? Well, they need to be ID3 tagged in the same way that music files have ID3 tags that tell us the title, artist, album, track number, or other information about the file, stored in the file itself. In the case of the podcast it is the title of the podcast, the originator, the name of the series if relevant and show notes that say a bit about the programme. Then the podcast will have to be RSS-enabled so that subscribers get new episodes when they are syndicated. Finally, they will need to be hosted on the web – they need to be permanently available on a dedicated third-party server for anyone who wants to download the podcast at any time. The good news is that much of this process can be automated.

The leading light in dedicated podcast syndication is libsyn (liberated syndication). If you create an account at www.libsyn.com it will guide you through the process of uploading and tagging your audio file and it will then host and syndicate the podcast for you. You can choose the aggregators that will distribute it. For some of these, iTunes in particular, there are some hurdles to overcome before your podcast will be listed.

There are many other ways of publishing podcasts. For example, a number of blogging programs will allow you to embed audio in your blog and also have the facility to syndicate. Once you have set up the feed the blog host will detect whenever you load audio into your blog and will syndicate it as a podcast. Where the podcast is embedded in the blog it is sometimes referred to as a blogcast.

Some organizations merely have podcasts on their websites available for streaming or as direct downloads, but these aren't podcasts in the true sense because they are not syndicated. Also, by definition you are limiting the audience to visitors to the site.

As with the section on podcast recording, this is the briefest guide to publishing your podcast. My advice here is the same: I would recommend calling in a professional rather than publishing the podcast yourself.

Vodcasts

It is just as easy to syndicate video as it is to publish a podcast. Setting aside for a moment the increased complexities in producing and editing both sound and vision there seems no reason why video podcasts or 'vodcasts' should not become as popular or indeed eclipse the popularity of their audio cousins. Steve Garfield, a former Boston-based radio producer and one of the internet's first video bloggers, launched his own video blog on 1 January 2004, with the declaration that 2004 would be the year of the video blog. It wasn't really and several years later the video blog still hasn't caught on.

I don't think we can actually set aside the production challenges that video sets. My very first job after university was in independent radio. I learned it was possible to produce really compelling programmes with just one or two people. A few years later, having moved into PR, I specialized in providing PR services to TV broadcasters and producers. I was astounded at just how many people it took to make a half-hour television programme and in many cases the programmes weren't even that compelling.

There is another challenge facing video blogs and vodcasts and that is the erosion of the traditional delivery systems for television. Now that we can get television from a variety of online sources including content aggregators like iTunes, the difference between a TV programme and a vodcast will disappear and the only distinction will be the quality of the content. As 'content is king' the winners in the video arena will emerge in the main from the television industry.

Social bookmarking

Social bookmarking is the Web 2.0 method of saving your internet favourites. Because it is a Web 2.0 evolution it means that the bookmarks you store, you also share. They can be kept private or you can choose to share them only with specified individuals or groups. Like the favourites in your web browser the bookmarks can be arranged chronologically, by category or by tags.

This allows the social bookmarking site to build information around the numbers of users who have selected a specific bookmark. The bookmarks can be rated and they can be imported or exported to and from browsers allowing you to access and store your favourites wherever you are.

A variety of social bookmarking sites came and went before the arrival of delicious (formerly del.icio.us) in 2003. Delicious introduced us to the idea of collaborative or social tagging, which in turn led to the idea of 'folksonomy', which is a kind of user-generated taxonomy (the science of classification). The site allows users to create their own tags for websites using freely chosen keywords, which means that over time and with increasing volumes of users the popular content on the internet becomes organized and categorized by its users. Similar sites like Furl and StumbleUpon followed soon after, as well as Digg and reddit, which have more of a news focus.

Social bookmarking systems offer a different way of organizing and searching content on the web from search engines that use automated programs known as web-bots or spiders to find content. These web classifications are created by human beings with intuition, as opposed to programs that use algorithms to attempt to determine what a site is about. In practice, people discover and bookmark web pages that have not yet been discovered or indexed by search engines.

Whilst we can't decide how many people will like the content that we publish and syndicate on the web or how much they will like it, we do need to be aware of sites like Digg and reddit and consider how we make our audience aware of the opportunity to use social bookmarking to raise interest in what we publish. The simplest way to do this is to provide links to these sites in the spaces that we create for the dissemination of our content, our websites, blogs and social media releases.

Social networking

The concept of social networking is the natural extension of the concept of the original internet. The precursor to the internet, the ARPANET (Advanced Research Projects Agency Network) was created in order to network a number of universities (see Chapter 1). The first basis for social networking that really caught the public's imagination was the means to re-establish contact with former schoolmates. Classmates.com was launched in the United States in 1995 and in a little over 10 years acquired over 40 million users. The UK equivalent, Friends Reunited, was launched in 2000, and in just five years gained 15 million users and a price tag of £120 million, the price that TV broadcaster ITV paid for it in 2000.

Social networks have evolved into online communities. The most popular social networking sites are being used by millions of people on a daily basis. They can be based around all sorts of things like friendship or common interests. As every day passes, the various ways for users to interact in social networks increases. They incorporate e-mail-style messaging and instant messaging (IM) or chat. They allow file sharing, blogging and often incorporate content from all sorts of other platforms such as those that publish video. Social networking is revolutionizing the way we communicate and share information. The most popular social networks, with around 200 million users between them at the time of writing, are MySpace and Facebook, with the latter growing at a faster rate and overtaking MySpace in terms of reach in April 2008.

Social networks are not just highly popular in terms of the number of users that they have and there is a very high level of engagement with the sites. This is one of the many reasons they have become of such interest to marketeers.

The Facebook phenomenon

In July 2008 Facebook had more than 80 million users. According to the major internet research companies Alexa and comScore, it was one of the top 10 most used sites on the web. It has become the leading photo-sharing application, with more than 14 million photos uploaded daily. Part of the reason for the variety of applications available through Facebook is the fact that it uses an open Application Programming Interface (API) in the form of the Facebook Platform, which gives developers access to produce applications for the Facebook community. By the middle of 2008 over 24,000 applications have been built on Facebook.

These statistics are all the more extraordinary given that Facebook was only made available to the general public in September 2006. Mark Zuckerberg founded 'The Facebook' in 2004 whilst a student at Harvard University. Membership was initially restricted to students of Harvard College. Within a month, over half of them had joined the site. Given the obvious popularity of the platform Zuckerberg made the site available to all of the Ivy League schools within a few months of the original launch. The following year a high school version was launched. Its popularity was immediate and the decision was taken to extend membership to businesses, with Apple and Microsoft employees amongst the first to be included. Facebook became open to anyone over the age of 13 on 26 September 2006. In a survey conducted amongst US students by Student Monitor in 2006, Facebook tied with 'drinking beer' for second place in a list of most popular things, with 71 per cent of the students identifying them as 'in' – most popular was the iPod.

Commercial interests that engage with social network sites should do so with great consideration and caution. This is an open environment where the audience can talk back and if they don't like what you're doing or saying they will say so. The most important thing to consider when planning a campaign that involves activity within a social network is whether you are able to give anything of any value to your audience through your participation. Simply promoting a commercial message will not be regarded as valuable. There are particular types of businesses and organizations whose presence on Facebook and other social network science would be better tolerated than others. Sectors that involve offline participation are going to work better in an area of online participation than those that don't. For example, sports clubs, music, fashion, leisure and even politics will be better suited to participation in social networks than oil companies or banks.

There are a number of things you can do with Facebook: you can list events, you can create a group, for example based around a particular area of interest, or you could work on developing an application. Potentially any of these things could generate significant interest but you should be cautious: Facebook itself is a huge and disparate place, and there are many examples of promotional activity that results in very little interest.

Social networks for stakeholder involvement

There are an increasing number of social networks that are built around interest groups or shared objectives or concerns. For some PR campaigns a dedicated social network might prove to be a particularly good way of communicating with stakeholders and delivering a hearts and minds campaign within a shared interest group. It is now possible to create your own social network. Ning is a platform where users can create their own social websites and social networks. It was co-founded by Marc Andreessen who was also the co-founder of Netscape. Ning is easy to use, and its features can be customized to upload pictures and videos. It can also be linked to other social networks such as the photo-sharing site it also carries, Google's open API, which will allow the incorporation of many future applications.

5 Digital PR and search engine optimization

Search is the dominant force on the web and content that ranks highly in a Google search is de facto going to have more hits, more impact and more value. There are currently six searches conducted via Google for every two on Yahoo! and one on Microsoft Live. PR practitioners therefore must take account of this and consider how they use digital PR to support good search rankings. PR activity is creating content that is of increasing relevance to the way that search engines work.

How search engine optimization evolved

As AltaVista, Yahoo!, Lycos and other early search engines began to rise to pre-eminence everybody involved in the internet became subject to the power and influence of search. At some time around the middle of the 1990s, the idea of search engine optimization (SEO) was spawned. In the early days, web designers submitted pages or links to all of the search engines and they in turn would send a web crawler to the site to collect information, which would then be indexed. The web crawler or spider would extract keywords that would provide the basis for future searches. Very quickly site owners and administrators started to work out ways of getting sites placed in searches, ideally as highly ranked as possible. This process by the end of the 1990s became known as search engine optimization.

Early searches relied on the information that was provided by the website itself in the form of tags or keywords. Content providers could manipulate these tags in an attempt to rank highly in searches. Search engines were going to have to improve the way that they found information or searching would become increasingly unreliable.

Two students at Stanford University, Larry Page and Sergey Brin, created a search engine technique based on mathematical algorithms that measured links from one website to another. This was the basis for Google, the search engine they launched in 1998. The search engine optimization business started to find ways to manipulate this new form of search. In short, they found ways of creating spurious links to the sites that they wanted to promote using devices such as link farms, which involved the creation of thousands of websites whose only function was to provide links to the original site to improve its page rank. SEO became an important element in any digital marketing campaign. SEO expanded to look at the actual functioning of the search algorithms and would review code, presentation and structure of websites to improve their ranking. All of the leading search engines, Google, Microsoft Search and Yahoo! use web crawlers to find pages automatically.

High page rankings can have a huge commercial value and therefore there continues to be a tension between the SEO business and optimal function of search engines. The techniques are regarded as being either good design that search engines approve of, or they are regarded as 'black hat' or attempts to trick search engines into providing a higher rank than a site actually merits. This will usually lead to these sites being banned temporarily or permanently once the search engines discover black hat techniques. For example using text that is hidden from human eyes but visible to a search engine. Some major international companies, such as BMW, have been accused of using some of these techniques and have been the subject of temporary bans by Google. As a way of dealing with this, the major search engine organizations have not only maintained the confidentiality of exactly how their searches work but they have also changed the processes on a regular basis.

In May 2007, Google introduced a radical change to the system by introducing the concept of 'universal search', which blends listings from its news, video, images, local and book search engines with those gathered from web crawlers. One of the changes is the use of vertical search, that is, if the search is about sport the search engine searches sports sites; if it is about a medical issue then medical sites will be promoted.

News, for example, works differently in universal search – the results are blended in with the traditional search results, which greatly elevates the importance of news stories in the search rankings for any commercial organization. Images and video are now also included in the main search.

Before the introduction of universal search, Google searches gave a list of 10 web results and things like news headlines did not appear (unless you used the separate and still available 'News' search) because of the way that the web search algorithms worked. Universal search changed this by running a simultaneous news search and blending the results.

PR and natural search

Natural search is a description of the process of searching that produces results based on their actual relevance rather than because their ranking has been boosted by paid-for search engine optimization techniques. The changes to the way that Google and other search engines operate is highly relevant for the public relations industry. In the first instance, it elevates the importance of news and PR is about news. The principal function of the public relations press office is to support journalists and to provide editorial content for news stories. To verify the importance of this, all you need to do is enter some search terms or the name of an organization that you are working for and you will see news content ranking highly in the Google first page results.

The other sources of content that are starting to rank highly in searches are the new channels that I covered in the previous chapter – blogs, wikis and podcasts. Social networks have become important in terms of creating searchable and relevant content. LinkedIn, the business-orientated social network, is a very good example. If you or someone you know has a LinkedIn profile try searching on a combination of the name and the name of the business where the person in question works. You should see the LinkedIn profile ranking highly in that search. If you think about it, most of us perform this type of search on a regular basis and usually whenever we are considering entering into any business partnership with someone new.

Having considered the increasing importance of public-relations-generated content we should give some thought to how we deliver that content in a way that is itself optimized for search. The public relations industry needs to start adopting some of the techniques that the white hat search engine optimizers have been using for years. For example, the type of language that we use in our written output needs to consider the use of terms that are more likely to be used when our audiences are using search engines. We will need to move away from the use of convoluted terms and phrases that in the past have been favoured by some branding campaigns to more straightforward and descriptive terminology that will raise our search rankings.

This is important as the industry moves away from the old-fashioned press release in favour of the more web-relevant social media release or SMR:

Google is not a search engine. Google is a reputation-manage-ment system, and that's one of the most powerful reasons so many CEOs have become more transparent: Online, your rep is quantifiable, findable, and totally unavoidable. In other words, radical transparency is a double-edged sword, but once you know the new rules, you can use it to control your image in ways you never could before. (Clive Thompson, *Wired* magazine, March 2007)

Social search

An article appeared in *Popular Mechanics* magazine in April 2008 that began with the words 'Search is dead'. The argument that the article posed was that the huge escalation in social networks would eventually make algorithm-based search engines redundant. This seems like a bold claim when Google has become arguably the world's most powerful brand, with a brand value of over $88 billion according to Millward Brown Optimor's BrandZ Top 100 Most Powerful Brands survey 2008. The core of the argument is that as sites like Facebook, MySpace, Twitter, Second Life, LinkedIn and Google's orkut grow, web users will find what they want by using their social network rather than search because they trust the people in their social network, or indeed people in general will know the answer that you want better than a mathematical equation. This is clearly starting to happen with micro-blogging. I'm currently following only 40 people on Twitter (although I've chosen to follow mainly people with expertise in the social web). In less that 24 hours I have seen a request from Jemima Kiss, technology writer for the *Guardian* and Tom Waits fan, for information about iTunes, and a request from social media guru Shel Israel for information on business applications on Twitter. Shel got what he wanted in just 10 minutes, admittedly quite a bit slower than Google but qualified by trusted human intelligence: 'shelisrael: Thanks everyone. I just got 10 good Twitter biz apps in 10 minutes. Keep them coming when you find them, please.'

Social networks or online communities are often built or reinforced around the notion of shared interests. We create an enormous amount of data when we participate in social networks according to the same article in *Popular Mechanics*:

Since we are essentially meta-tagging ourselves through our social networking memberships, shopping habits and surfing addictions, it's conceivable that the information could attempt to find us – the old concept of push media, but in a far more refined way. As new content enters the Web, it could tumble through the various filters that you set up around your identity and then show up on your home-page newsfeed, or in your

in box, or pop up on a ticker that follows you around as you
browse from page to page.

The principles of the social web have crossed over into algorithmic
search. Launched in mid-2008, Scour is a social search engine that
combines the searches from three popular search engines as well
as allowing users to vote on the results. Scour takes results from
Google, Yahoo! and Live Search by searching and ranking the
results dependent on the recommendations of its users. It is also
possible to customize Scour and filter by any combination of the
three search engines. The user-generated aspect of the Scour search
means that the user gives a search result a 'thumbs up' if it is relevant
or a 'thumbs down' if it isn't. Votes and comments directly impact
on the search rankings. Scour also includes a rewards system where
users collect points for searching, commenting and voting as well
as inviting friends to the site. Scour points can then be cashed in
for money in the form of Visa vouchers. According to the site itself
'Scour's purpose is to bridge the gap between searchers and relevant
results. By providing a platform for the user to vote and comment on
relevancy, searchers connect with one another creating a true social
search community.'

6 The power of the new media

The change in the nature of influence means that there will be new winners and losers. Commercial success will be driven more by customer service and utility than by ideas of brand personality. In an environment where organizations can no longer closely control the media and the message, the real customer experience carries enormous importance.

We have already seen the growth of brands that reflect these qualities. In the 2008 edition of Millward Brown Optimor's BrandZ Top 100 Most Powerful Brands survey, the biggest climber with an increase in brand value of 390 per cent is BlackBerry. This is a brand entirely built around utility – providing its customers with a new way to keep in touch, and ultimately an improved way in which to do business.

The company that makes the BlackBerry, RIM (Research in Motion), identified a need that was poorly served by existing technology: the need to receive and send e-mail when away from the office or even just away from your desk. It was a simple concept that took a few short years to revolutionize corporate life. Executives are so drawn to the device that some describe their reliance as an addiction – hence the popular moniker 'crackberry'.

RIM also demonstrates that it is in touch with the zeitgeist by including a section on Corporate Philanthropy alongside Contact

Information, Executive Biographies, RIM Press Releases and Investor Relations on the Company page of its corporate website.

The Scrabulous story

There is a story that demonstrates the scale and commercial value of some of the new channels on the web. It involves Facebook and one of the world's best-loved and most enduring board games. It is a story that shows how the rule book can be thrown away and even how long-standing legal frameworks can be challenged.

The story begins in India in 2005. Two brothers, Rajat and Jayant Agarwalla, both commerce graduates of St Xavier's College, Kolkata and devoted Scrabble enthusiasts, decide that the game would lend itself to an online version. They create the first iteration at BingoBinge. com. On the BingoBinge website the game is described as online Scrabble. They changed the name to Scrabulous and launched it on Scrabulous.com in July 2006. In an echo of what happened when the original board game gained exposure when it went on sale in Macy's department store, interest in Scrabulous rocketed and the game went global when it was launched as an application on Facebook in May 2007. Conservative estimates suggest that within a year there were 0.5 million people playing Scrabulous every day. That is a quite staggering statistic but it gains considerable perspective when you consider that the inventor of Scrabble, Alfred Butts, took 17 years from inventing the game to finding a manufacturer. Ironically, one of his biggest hurdles was registering a patent, with the US patent office initially denying it.

For those of you unfamiliar with Scrabulous it is virtually indistinguishable from Scrabble, except that it is an online version. The rules are the same, the board looks the same, the composition of the letters is the same; it appears that nobody disputes that it is the same game.

You would expect then, some interest from the company, or in this case companies, that own the rights to distribute and sell Scrabble: Hasbro, which has exclusive rights to the North American market, and Mattel, which markets Scrabble in all markets outside the United States. For six months they did nothing.

In January 2008, they acted for the first time. Scrabulous was denounced for online piracy and Rajat and Jayant Agarwalla were threatened with legal action by Hasbro and Mattel. But then strangely nothing happened. There were no writs, no court cases, no instructions to cease and desist and more importantly Scrabulous remained on Facebook. What did happen was that there was an outcry amongst Scrabulous players on Facebook. A 'Save Scrabulous' group gained nearly 50,000 members and there were even online threats to boycott Hasbro and Mattel products.

Three months later I had the good fortune to be invited to a talk by Facebook's UK commercial director, Blake Chandlee, held at the offices of advertising agency TBWA\Manchester. In the interests of full disclosure I ought to add that this was shortly before I joined TBWA\'s PR company Staniforth\. I asked Blake about Scrabulous and whether he thought that either Hasbro or Mattel would pursue legal action over the matter. He stated quite clearly that he thought they would not.

We must ask ourselves why, given that this seems to be a very clear breach of copyright, the owners did not immediately act to protect their intellectual property. There are a number of clues. Neither Hasbro nor Mattel will confirm how many Scrabble games they have sold since Scrabulous started becoming popular. In a normal year Hasbro claims that it will sell between 1 and 2 million. That is less than the number of players enjoying the online version in a single week. Could it be that Scrabulous is actually driving interest and sales for the original product? We don't know because they won't tell us. Writing in the *Guardian*, in July 2008, Oliver Burkeman reports that 'It seems inconceivable that the games companies would want to alienate such a vast number of Scrabble enthusiasts – some of whom have doubtless bought physical sets as a result of playing Scrabulous – so the logical solution would be for a deal to be reached.'

Let's consider for a moment the first quarter performance for Hasbro in 2008. Here is an extract from the highlights in its first quarter statement:

- net revenues of $704.2 million, an increase of $78.9 million or 13 per cent compared to $625.3 million a year ago, or an increase of 9 per cent after the impact of foreign exchange;
- net earnings of $37.5 million, or $0.25 per diluted share, compared to $32.9 million, or $0.19 per diluted share last year.

So how was that growth achieved? According to Alfred J. Verrecchia, President and Chief Executive Officer, 'we had a strong 2007 and the momentum continues in 2008, with growth driven primarily by TRANSFORMERS and LITTLEST PET SHOP, as well as PLAYSKOOL, STAR WARS, BABY ALIVE, MY LITTLE PONY and board games'.

I am very intrigued as to why he says 'and board games' without saying which board games and yet he refers to all of the other products by name – indeed even using capital letters . To my knowledge, and I spent many years with clients in the toy and games industries, board games haven't been a serious engine of growth since Trivial Pursuit over a quarter of a century ago.

So let's assume that even an unbranded version of a board game that works online within a powerful social network can drive real growth and interest in the original product. Rather than sue for breach of copyright at the time at which the transgression occurred you might allow the situation to continue and build a following for as long as it took to develop an official version, which could then be launched in the same environment. That is exactly what happened.

In early July 2008 Electronic Arts announced that it had created an official Hasbro-licensed and endorsed version of Scrabble, which it launched on Facebook the same month. The Electronic Arts version contains features that Scrabulous doesn't have like dynamic animations. Because the EA version is licensed by Hasbro and not Mattel it was only available to Facebook users in the United States and Canada. It has another drawback – on Facebook, although Hasbro actually owns the original copyright, as far as playing Scrabble on a social network is concerned this new 'official' version is a copycat or 'me too' application because Scrabulous got there first. Gary Serby, a spokesperson for Hasbro, said in a statement at the time of the launch: 'Hasbro has been consistent in stating that Scrabulous infringes upon our intellectual property, and we are keeping our legal options open. Today we are focusing on the coming launch of

EA's legitimate social networking version of Scrabble. We have no further comment.'

Facebook users were almost universal in the opposition and condemnation of attempts to bring officially licensed versions of the board game to the social network environment. Here is a post from a Celia Barker in London on 10 July 2008:

> It should not be beyond the wit and wisdom of two major companies to develop a solution to the geographical copyright situation if they wish to get onto the internet. The world has moved on and they should move with it rather than impose their business model in a way that alienates their target customers. The guys that developed Scrabulous have done more to promote Scrabble than either Hasbro or Mattel have done in the past 40 years. I've been around all that time so I speak from personal observation.

My personal view was that Blake Chandlee's opinion was right; that it made little sense for Hasbro or Mattel to go through with their threatened legal action because they had too little to gain and too much to lose. However, on Thursday 24 July 2008 Hasbro filed a lawsuit in the New York district court against Facebook and Scrabulous, alleging copyright infringement under the Digital Millennium Copyright Act. Elliot Schrage, Facebook's Vice President for Communications and Public Policy, said that:

> games are an important part of the social experience on Facebook. Our hope and expectation is that the parties can resolve their disagreements in a manner that satisfies the parties, that continues to offer a great experience to gamers and that doesn't discourage other developers from using [the Facebook] platform to share their creativity and test new ideas... We're disappointed that Hasbro has sought to draw us into their dispute.

From a legal point of view the case of copyright infringement is not quite as clear as it might be. 'The idea of Scrabble, the idea that you would get points for spelling words, can't be copyrighted,' said James

M Burger, a partner at the Washington law firm Dow Lohnes. 'The only thing you can copyright is the look and the feel of the game.'

A week later, Facebook removed Scrabulous in the United States and then briefly removed it in the United Kingdom before reinstating it for UK users a day later. It became very clear that both Facebook and the Agarwalla brothers had been preparing for this eventuality. A day after the removal of Scrabulous, a new game had appeared on Facebook that bore a considerable resemblance to its predecessor. Wordscraper had been developed by Rajat and Jayant in the months preceding the legal action. It uses round tiles rather than square ones, and the board uses a different arrangement of double word, double and triple letter squares. This aspect of the game is also customizable, so effectively, if the user wants to recreate the original Scrabble board layout, they could easily do so.

Doris Long, a professor of intellectual property law at the University of Chicago's John Marshall Law School, said that Wordscraper had a good chance of passing the legal test:

> But by giving the power to the end users to control the design of the board, including presumably the ability to change the board design back to the Scrabulous design, Hasbro could still pursue a contributory infringement claim if it wanted to under the 'active inducement' test... But to win, Hasbro would have to show that the designers actively encouraged gamers to change the board back to the old Scrabulous. So far they don't seem to be stepping over this line.

No doubt both Facebook and Rajat and Jayant Agarwalla took extensive legal advice as to how to differentiate the game sufficiently from Scrabble in order to avoid further action, or significantly strengthen their position in the event that Hasbro pursued action against Wordscraper. Hasbro responded to the launch of Wordscraper with a terse statement:

> Hasbro has an obligation to protect its intellectual property and will act appropriately when necessary. We recently filed a lawsuit against the developers of the infringing Scrabulous application, and we are pleased that the unlawful application

has been removed from Facebook. We evaluate every situation on a case-by-case basis and have no comment regarding the Scrabulous developers' new application at this time.

Within a week Wordscraper had attracted 100,000 users. Scrabulous had been effectively replaced and its loss would not have a measurable impact on Facebook usage, the Agarwalla's had successfully migrated their version of the game into a format that they could more effectively promote and gained a massive amount of publicity at the same time. By the weekend following the launch of Wordscraper, Google was returning 1,000 news items and over 50,000 searches in total for the term 'Wordscraper'. Hasbro generated quite a bit of bad feeling amongst the half-million-plus players on Facebook. It also seems unlikely that a game with a name that is unfamiliar and an onscreen board that looks much less like its counterpart will translate so readily into sales of Scrabble.

This outcome was no longer quite such a major issue for Facebook. The game had driven interest in the network and involved its users (as well as no doubt shifting a fair number of Scrabble boards for the copyright owners). More important for Mark Zuckerberg and his team was the new Facebook Connect (which allows users to connect their Facebook identity, friends and privacy to any site), announced a few days before Hasbro filed its lawsuit in the New York courts, and the next major step forward for the social networking behemoth.

7 The new ethics

The public relations industry has never been particularly celebrated for its ethics. In fact, we PR people are right up there with politicians and journalists in terms of how our honesty is perceived. To some extent, we only have ourselves to blame and in part it is because we allow the line between public relations advisers and publicists to become blurred. Public relations is a strategic marketing discipline, whereas publicity is a rather more straightforward activity. In some cases, both publicists and journalists have gone along with the old maxim never to let the truth get in the way of a good story. There is undoubtedly an unholy alliance that allows certain journalists to write things that they know are untrue because a publicist has told them that is so.

Many years ago I found myself sitting next to the celebrated British publicist, Max Clifford, at an industry lunch in Manchester at which he was the guest speaker. He had been responsible for bringing about the public disgrace of the British government minister, David Mellor. Max Clifford revealed that David Mellor was having an affair with a little-known actress called Antonia de Sancha. Clifford had touted the story that Mellor, a well-known Chelsea football fan, had asked the actress to make love to him whilst he was dressed in his Chelsea football shirt. The story made the front page of the *Sun* newspaper. During lunch, I took the opportunity to ask Mr Clifford whether the story had in fact been true. He laughed and admitted it was a total fabrication. He added that he had tried the same tactic with the colourful left-wing labour politician, Derek Hatton, five years earlier. That time the story was 'leaked' to the press entirely with the politician's consent as a way of getting publicity in order to raise his profile in advance of a hoped-for TV career. The other principal difference was that Derek Hatton was a Liverpool fan. The story didn't make the front page but according to Clifford it did appear in the *Sun*. After lunch and after Clifford had given a short address, questions were thrown open to the floor and a guest asked the same question that I had. Bizarrely, Clifford responded by saying that he didn't know if the story was true 'but who would you believe' he asked, spinning for Britain, 'David Mellor or Antonia?'

The old ethics

Many outsiders have regarded PR as a profession without an ethical core but this is not the case. The professional bodies that represent the PR industry codify the requirement for honest and ethical behaviour in the conduct of their members. The largest representative body for PR professionals in the United States, the Public Relations Society of America (PRSA) and the Chartered Institute of Public Relations (CIPR) in the United Kingdom both require ethical and honest behaviour from their members. The PRSA has a Code of Ethics that contains the following advice in its preamble:

> The Public Relations Society of America (PRSA) is committed to ethical practices. The level of public trust PRSA members seek, as we serve the public good, means we have taken on a special obligation to operate ethically.
>
> The value of member reputation depends upon the ethical conduct of everyone affiliated with the Public Relations Society of America. Each of us sets an example for each other – as well as other professionals – by our pursuit of excellence with powerful standards of performance, professionalism, and ethical conduct.

Within the Code itself, which members are expected to sign, it contains the following advice:

> A member shall:
> Preserve the integrity of the process of communication.
> Be honest and accurate in all communications.

The preamble to the Code of Conduct for the CIPR in the United Kingdom contains similar invocations:

> The Code emphasizes that honest and proper regard for the public interest; reliable and accurate information; and never misleading clients, employers and other professionals about the nature of representation or what can be competently delivered or achieved, arc vital components of robust professional practice.

The Code itself begins with the principles of good practice, which enshrine the need for honesty and integrity, to which its members must agree:

> Members of the Chartered Institute of Public Relations agree to:
>
> Maintain the highest standards of professional endeavour, integrity, confidentiality, financial propriety and personal conduct;
> Deal honestly and fairly in business with employers, employees, clients, fellow professionals, other professions and the public.

It goes on to add:

> Fundamental to good public relations practice are:
> Integrity;
> Honest and responsible regard for the public interest;
> Checking the reliability and accuracy of information before dissemination.

It is true to say that not all public relations practitioners belong to a professional body and that some members of these bodies do not adhere to their codes but it has been the case for as long as the PR industry has existed that most of its practitioners are adherents to the importance of ethical practice.

At the same time, the industry has had to deal with the concept of 'spin'. Spin usually implies a highly selective presentation of the facts in order to turn news coverage into something more favourable for an organization or client that the 'spin doctor' represents. Whilst traditional public relations allows for advocacy and a considerable role for presentation, 'spin' tends to be regarded as deceptive and manipulative – selectively providing facts or opinions that support a particular position and hiding those that don't.

The term came to prominence during election campaigns in the United Kingdom and the United States during the 1990s and it has been most commonly used to describe the activities of press advisors working for politicians. Perhaps the most infamous use of spin in the United Kingdom was when government advisor, Jo Moore, advised her press office immediately after the bombings of 11 September 2001 that it was a good day to bury bad news. She sent an e-mail that stated: 'It's now a very good day to get out anything we want to bury.' There was unsurprisingly something of an uproar when this was reported in the press. This and similar events that followed eventually caused her to resign. The United Kingdom's most famous 'spin doctor' was Alastair Campbell, who was regarded by most to be Prime Minister Tony Blair's most important advisor between 1994 and 2003. He was directly responsible for the Prime Minister's media relations. His tenure charts a fundamental shift in the public attitude to spin.

In the early 1990s, 'spin' was hardly even considered to be a pejorative term. In 1998 my old friend Andy Spinoza, a former journalist, set up a PR company called Spin Media. It was regarded by most as a clever use of a popular term and it had also been Andy's childhood nickname. It was and is a very successful PR company. In a press release issued in December 2005 announcing a change of name to Spinoza Kennedy Vesey Public Relations, Andy or rather Andrew, was quoted as saying:

In 1998, 'spin' was taken to mean dynamic and smart, now it has a range of negative associations. As the agency has grown, including delivering public sector campaigns for government agencies and local authorities, we need to present ourselves in a way which reflects our key attributes: intelligence, integrity, creativity and delivery... The original name has outlived its usefulness and the change marks a new phase in the agency's evolution.

One branch of public relations that has always had a powerful ethical stance is the function of crisis and issues communications. By definition a crisis is an unexpected situation or event likely to be detrimental to a brand or organization – this may range from something as simple as serious customer dissatisfaction through to a major disaster. All of the leading exponents agree that organizations facing such a situation should: respond quickly, deal openly and honestly with the media and avoid at all costs taking a 'no comment' stance. It is also critically important that the organization acknowledges the crisis, quickly seeks to identify the cause and responsibilities and takes the appropriate action to acknowledge responsibility and provide an explanation of what it intends to do to resolve matters. Failure to do this will lead very rapidly to public anxiety or anger and this will quickly become the focus of media coverage.

One reason for the emphasis on truth and openness in a crisis is the high level of media interest that a crisis will generate. Quite simply if an organization tries to spin in this situation the presence and involvement of a significant number of journalists means that it will be found out. This will happen quickly and the negative news coverage will spiral out of control. In some cases the organization will never recover. The pressure and intensity of the media focus is the key here.

In many ways the old-fashioned crisis is a good proxy for the environment we increasingly find ourselves in every day. The rise of citizen journalism means that the focus on organizations is ever present. There are more eyes on our organizations and if they don't deal honestly there is more likelihood that they will be found out.

The new ethics and enlightened self-interest

In this newly defined environment, organizations quite simply have no place to hide. They are constantly under scrutiny and their customers are able to talk back. Where in the past a customer who was dissatisfied with a product or service might need to deal with the complexities of a customer complaints department they can now express their dissatisfaction in a very public fashion by starting or contributing to a blog.

Since the dawn of the era of user-generated content (UGC) there have been some very celebrated examples of businesses that have caused themselves very public embarrassment. Wal-Mart, the US shopping giant, has come unstuck a number of times. It was exposed for altering its Wikipedia entry in 2005, which included removing the entry that referred to its wages being lower than other retail chains and adding the statement that it pays nearly double the minimum wage to its staff.

The following year a blog appeared called 'Wal-Marting Across America'. It was supposedly the travelogue of 'Jim and Laura', an ordinary couple who were touring across the United States in an RV and parking for free in Wal-Mart car parks at night. In their first post they state 'We are not bloggers, but… we figured we'd give it a go.' Along the way they met various Wal-Mart employees and needless to say these were all positive experiences. The blog also reinterpreted the term 'Wal-Marting', which was normally used in a pejorative way to describe how large dominant retail chains crush small local retailers with the long-term effect of making every town look the same.

It turned out that the blog was a fabrication or at the very least it was highly distorted as a result of the fact that it was funded by Wal-Mart via their public relations advisers Edelman, who came up with the idea in the first place. Suffice to say that Wal-Mart and Edelman were exposed, and the golden rule is that you always will be, and then forced to make a public apology. They had ignored the first rule of digital marketing and that is the principle of full disclosure. Always say who you are and what your interest is in the subject at hand or someone else is very likely to do it for you.

Wal-Mart is not the only major company that has been accused of using fake blogs, or 'flogs' as they are called in some quarters.

When Microsoft was launching Vista, it decided that it was going to be essential to get bloggers talking about the new operating system. It decided that the best way to do this was to send free advance copies of Vista to influential bloggers. Quite a reasonable idea you might think but it decided to send out brand new laptops to go along with the system. Microsoft argued that this was to ensure that none of the bloggers attempted to load the OS onto old machines that would not work properly with Vista. There was a huge outcry amongst the bloggers. They plugged in their brand new laptops and used them to publish blogs that said that Microsoft was bribing them with the new laptops in return for good reviews. Microsoft claimed that this was not so and suggested that the laptops could be sent back or auctioned for charity, but the damage was already done.

It shouldn't have been hard for Edelman to understand the appropriate and ethical manner in which they might have gone about following Jim and Laura on a trip around the United States. After all, the agency's president and CEO, Richard Edelman, helped to craft the code of ethics for the Word of Mouth Marketing Association (WOMMA). Public relations professionals have an increasing number of places to turn to for ethical advice. The Chartered Institute of Public Relations (CIPR) has a specific Code of Ethics to cover participation in social media.

The CIPR Code identifies a number of issues such as 'astroturfing' (see Chapter 4), which is the practice of falsely creating the impression of popular grassroots support. Although this is not something exclusive to the web, it has been spurred on by the arrival of UGC. The concept of full disclosure is important here because if you clearly identify who you are, you can't 'astroturf'. The Code also covers some of the issues when it comes to pitching to bloggers and its associations with spamming. Like any good PR approach, if we do our research and understand individual bloggers' interests we will avoid being ignored or blocked. Full disclosure in this area of engagement is again important if we want to ensure that the positive interest isn't followed by critical posts about your PR company or even your client.

Whilst the social web makes our work infinitely more complex it provides us with the opportunity in the medium term to rid the PR industry of its unethical practitioners. It forces practitioners to operate more ethically even if it is just through enlightened self-interest.

The wider impact

The impact on ethics is not limited to the way we ply our trade; it impacts directly on how our clients, and indeed all organizations and businesses, conduct themselves. Businesses need to conduct themselves ethically because they will be held responsible for their actions whether or not the people at the top of the organization are aware of the malpractice.

A good example of this was the situation that one of the world's biggest advertising and marketing groups found itself in during the appalling events surrounding the fraudulent re-election of President Robert Mugabe in Zimbabwe. WPP, which owns several public relations agencies including Cohn & Wolfe, GCI, Hill & Knowlton, Burson-Marsteller and Ogilvy Public Relations Worldwide, discovered that it had a 25 per cent stake in an advertising company run by Mugabe's daughter, an agency that was involved in key elements of the election campaign. WPP issued a statement with great haste in order to demonstrate the organization's principles:

WPP statement on Zimbabwe
25 June, 2008

WPP shares the world's outrage at what is happening in Zimbabwe.

We were therefore extremely alarmed by the allegation last week that a firm in which we hold a minority interest (25 per cent) through Y&R and over which we have no legal control, may be advising Robert Mugabe and his political party. This could never happen with our knowledge or approval and we investigated the situation as a matter of urgency.

We have now established that a senior member of the management had been advising President Mugabe in a personal capacity. Nonetheless we want no association with this effort.

WPP's board and management have established clear guidelines for our operating companies on clients for which we are prepared to work. The Mugabe regime in Zimbabwe is not an acceptable client in accordance with these standards.

The decision to divest Y&R's minority interests in Zimbabwe was proposed earlier this year and we are working to ensure this is completed as soon as possible.

The rise of citizen journalism should provide positive sustainable benefits for society as a whole. It is reasonable to assume that it will bring pressure to support the continued ascent of ethical business practice. New, more ethical, businesses will emerge and existing businesses will become more ethical even if they are not driven by altruism but simply by the knowledge that it is in their interests to do so.

The significance of ethics in a world of empowered conversations was identified a decade ago with the seminal text *The Cluetrain Manifesto*, written in 1999 by Rick Levine, Christopher Locke, Doc Searls and David Weinberger. The book begins with the following pronouncement:

A powerful global conversation has begun. Through the internet, people are discovering and inventing new ways to share relevant knowledge with blinding speed. As a direct result, markets are getting smarter – and getting smarter faster than most companies. These markets are conversations. Their members communicate in language that is natural, open, honest, direct, funny and often shocking. Whether explaining or complaining, joking or serious, the human voice is unmistakably genuine. It can't be faked.

8 The blurring of channels

All branches of the media are becoming infinitely more complex and at the same time the distinctions between them are being eroded. Taking the example of television, we have had an explosion of conventional channels. At one time a particular programme or series was only ever televised on a single channel, now the same programme may appear on several channels. A quarter of a century ago all of the channels were broadcast from transmitters and received through aerials. Now there are a myriad of satellite and cable channels. We don't even need a television to watch television any more. In fact, using a PC to watch television allows for a much more flexible experience. Using systems like iTunes, the BBC's iPlayer, Hulu, Joost or Babelgum means that you can watch what you want, when you want and you can schedule your own evening's viewing. Emily Bell, the Director of Digital Content at the *Guardian*, has for a number of years been forecasting the end of the linear television. Its demise is well and truly upon us. The end of linear television also means the demise of traditional broadcast channels. This means that we are seeking out programmes rather than channels.

This blurring of the lines doesn't stop with television linearity. Consider the social networking site Bebo. It is moving from being simply a social network to becoming a major distributor of television and video content. Not only is it distributing content from traditional

TV broadcasters and other content providers but it is creating its own highly successful TV series. A teenage soap called *Kate Modern* was launched in July 2007. It had 155 mini-episodes, each lasting between one and four minutes. It attracted an average of 1.5 million viewers per week. It was so successful that Bebo commissioned two more online series – *Sofia's Diary* and *The Gap Year. Sofia's Diary* attracted 5 million viewers in its first two weeks on Bebo. It achieved a major goal by becoming the first online show to be bought by a traditional major broadcaster. Five bought the rights for its digital television channel.

Radio stations have started broadcasting video feeds via their websites. Magazines have launched TV channels. Major newspapers like the *Guardian* are producing very sophisticated radio content and these series are available as podcasts. Other newspapers are adding video clips to their websites as a way of enriching the content.

Integration through disintegration

It is received wisdom that integrated marketing is far more effective than attempting to reach your audience by using a single channel. Messages that come from a single source will have less credibility than similar messages that come from multiple sources. In addition, the opportunity for mass marketing is diminishing in line with the fall in audiences for all the major media channels. The American Marketing Association describes integrated marketing as 'a planning process designed to assure that all brand contacts received by a customer or prospect for a product, service, or organization are relevant to that person and consistent over time'.

The blurring of channels means that there are far more sources of information and places where brand contacts might be made. The buzzword of the moment is fragmentation. In a way, media channels are disintegrating. The 'long tail' (see Chapter 4) means that there are more and more routes to smaller and more narrowly defined groups of people.

This disintegration is most keenly observed on the web where choice and variety are expanding exponentially. Although the web is disparate and fragmented it has structure at its very core. The concept of linking from one web space to another allows us to drive new forms of integration. Whatever the nature of the digital PR campaign we deliver we should pay close attention to linking the various elements together as far as we are able. There are a number of things we can do to make this happen. In our communications with the media, be that by e-mail or through social media releases, we should contain links not just to places that we own such as the client's main website but all sorts of other places that might be of interest or that are relevant to the story we are trying to promote. First, this is helpful to the journalist and second, where we are generating online coverage, some of these links may be included, which in turn raises the likelihood that these sites will link back to us – a process some call 'link love'. By increasing the links to and from the content that we have influenced we increase the number and the relevance of the brand contacts that our target audience experiences.

It's the content not the channel

We are moving away from a world where content and products were pushed to a world in which content and products are pulled. There are many reasons for this and they are all interlinked. The decline of deference means that the consumer is less willing to accept what is being pushed. In the digital landscape it is easy and quick to tailor content to consumer demand. Even in manufacturing and production we are seeing an increasing number of bespoke processes and offers.

Media channels are all about push marketing. You decide which channel suits you, be that a TV broadcast channel or a daily newspaper, and once you've chosen you accept the content thereafter that is pushed to you. The ability to pick and choose content from lots of different sources means that we don't have to accept what is being pushed. As we schedule our own content, from TV viewing to the consumption of news, our choices and interests override those of schedulers and editors.

This elevation of consumer choice will separate the wheat from the chaff. The phrase 'content is king' becomes increasingly relevant. People seek out content that is relevant to them, which contains something of genuine interest, which engages them some other way, for example through humour, or which provides genuine and powerful insight.

As PR communicators we need to be very careful about content. Historically, we have a tendency to feel that if something is published then our goals have been achieved. The ease with which things can now be published undermines that presumption. The sheer volume of web content means that that which has no interest will have no impact. There is simply too much out there and many sites and pages will quite literally never be viewed by anyone other than their originators. For print media, cost is a barrier to entry, which means that there needs to be a sufficient audience in order to generate revenue to keep the publication afloat. What that meant was that if we achieved coverage in a niche publication there would still be some relevance and in almost every case we could quantify the circulation and readership and understand certain things about people who were reading the title.

We must not allow ourselves to be fooled by the idea that if we have something published on the web that guarantees us an audience. It is similar to the old argument that it is not sufficient simply to measure column inches. Fortunately there are many tools at our disposal to measure what is going on on the web and the impact and authority of individual web spaces and these will be examined in more detail in a later chapter.

There is a great danger that as we start to optimize our copy with keywords we forget the most important thing: the copy still needs to be well written and interesting. It is astonishing how often this is forgotten in the rush to upload. Interesting and engaging content has a direct impact on search engine rankings and consequently on traffic. Some traditional websites sacrifice the need for good written content because their search engine optimization (see Chapter 5) advisors have influenced keywords and their placement in the text to such an extent that the site no longer informs or entertains. What this process fails to acknowledge is that the quality of the content is critical to receiving high rankings, because it will affect the number of pages viewed and the stickiness of the site. Crafting words is a core skill for the majority of PR people but we also need to consider how to deliver quality content in all of its other forms – still images, audio and video. Whilst using the agency or in-house digital camera is useful for the odd application, for important work we will still tend to use a professional photographer. The same should apply for audio and video content. Where content is king we should engage professionals to help us deliver the best possible and most relevant audio and visual content that we can.

There are some trends in consuming content that we should be aware of. One of these is the notion of cyber-balkanization or the division of the internet into narrowly focused groups of like-minded individuals who have little involvement with outsiders. In terms of news consumption this means that they will tend to go back to the same places for information. This is similar to the idea of reading the same newspaper every day and therefore I don't think it should concern us too deeply. It is well to be aware of it and there are some very clear signs of traditional media organizations reinventing themselves as online brands or communities. They have succeeded in building on the trust that they achieved as traditional news organizations and redeploying that in a digital environment. Some good examples of this are the *New York Times*, the *Daily Telegraph* and *Guardian* newspapers and the BBC.

In addition to behavioural trends we are seeing the emergence of some very sophisticated content aggregators that assist people in finding content that is of interest to them. Last.fm, now owned by CBS, is a very good, if simple, early example that learns people's musical tastes and creates the equivalent of a radio station that is personally tailored to their tastes. A more recent and more sophisticated example is The Filter, which is described as a recommendation engine. The concept was developed originally by Peter Gabriel, the Grammy award-winning solo artist, former member of rock band Genesis and digital media pioneer. The Filter works a little like Last. fm but it covers a much wider range of online entertainment and information. It uses unique algorithms to deliver entertainment content: music and film video, as well as news and reviews that are tailored to an individual's tastes. In addition to using a search engine that monitors behaviour you can set The Filter to process tastes of people whose recommendations you value – for example, a well-known radio DJ or maybe a good friend who somehow always manages to come across good music before anyone else. 'The Filter aims to be the best possible blend of man and machine – a hybrid engine that filters all entertainment content to one's own personal taste,' says Martin Hopkins, a co-founder and CSO of The Filter.

Human beings require structure and we are seeing new structures emerge on the internet that are created around content rather that channels. In fact, we no longer need a channel to deliver content because we can create new channels in the form of blogs or micro-sites with consummate ease. Marshall McLuhan was a Canadian philosopher and a professor of English literature, who rose to prominence in the 1960s as a renowned expert and theorist in media and communications. He observed the impact of mass media communications and originally coined the phrase the 'global village'. Marshall McLuhan was also responsible for another culturally significant observation. In his book *Understanding Media: The Extensions of Man,* published in 1964, McLuhan argues that media themselves, not the content they carry, should be the focus of our attention and that the characteristics of the media are more significant and influential than their content. He proclaimed that 'the medium is the message'. In this new era of communications the natural laws have reasserted themselves and the message is now the medium.

9 The battle for influence at the digital frontier

Whenever we human beings find ourselves in a new environment there is a struggle for power and control. The fact that this environment is virtual rather than physical makes very little difference. Because this is new territory all sorts of different people are staking a claim to knowledge, understanding and influence. In the area of marketing communications, which is the area that is of most interest to you and me, a fierce debate is playing out as to which traditional marketing disciplines are best suited to the new conditions created by a digital world to which everybody has access. The traditional powerhouses of the marketing industry have been the large advertising agencies. Many of these agencies recognize that the era of single message mass marketing is coming to an end.

In a presentation to 250 marketing and advertising executives in New York on 6 November 2007, Facebook founder and CEO, Mark Zuckerberg, told the audience, 'for the last hundred years media has been pushed out to people, but now marketers are going to be a part of the conversation and they're going to do this by using the social graph in the same way our users do'.

A few of these big agencies are successfully reinventing themselves. TBWA\, regarded by many as one of the most creative of the larger advertising groups, has added the concept of 'media arts', an approach to an evolving media landscape, to the process of 'disruption'. This is a proprietary discipline that places a challenge to market conventions at the heart of the agency's creative process. Doing so allows the agency group to develop campaigns appropriate to the new environment. At this point, in the interests of full disclosure, I should remind you that I work for an agency that is part of the TBWA\ group.

Many of the larger agencies have been too slow to come to the realization that we live in a changing world. Many of these behemoths are locked into organizational structures designed for a passing age and will find it difficult to adapt.

The third wave of online influence

I believe that we have now entered a third phase since the inception of digital marketing. The first phase was a technical one, the second was built around design and creativity and this third phase is characterized by the democratization of content. Let me explain in a little more detail.

In the mid to late 1990s when businesses first launched commercial websites there were no tools available that allowed anyone other than a programmer or coder to build a website. Basically, unless you were familiar with HTML you could not build a website. The industry therefore was totally reliant on technicians. Specialist agencies sprang up and clients were in their thrall. It was common for agency account managers and client marketing directors to sit through meetings, understanding little of what was being said and placing their trust entirely in the hands of digital specialists.

Over a period of time, coding became more commoditized and various tools and programs became available that allowed the less technical to do more and more. At this stage the creative and design community starts to be able to exert more of an influence. The look and feel as well as the functionality of a website became more important. In this second phase designers and creatives, especially those with some technical understanding, gained pre-eminence in the field of digital marketing.

With the arrival of this third wave of digital communications, characterized by user-generated content (UGC), templated design has become more prevalent. More importantly, much of what we see on screen is originated in a space beyond the control of clients or agencies. Now the content comes from lots of different places, the skills that are important to the marketing function are not hard technical skills, nor are they predominantly aesthetic but are the softer management skills of diplomacy and influence. In short, these are the skills that PR people have always used in their interactions with traditional media.

Why the time has come for PR 2.0

I strongly believe that we are on the cusp of a very important era for the public relations industry. We can no longer buy influence in the way that we previously could. The movement away from traditional advertising techniques has been forecast for some time. Technical advances like TiVo, the first hard disk recording system that allowed viewers to skip though TV advertising, have been around for a decade. In 2002, two books were published that foreshadowed some of the changes that we are now starting to see: *The Fall of Advertising & the Rise of PR* by Ries and Ries and *The End of Advertising as We Know It* by Sergio Zyman, the former chief marketing officer of Coca-Cola. Neither of these books was about the changes arising from Web 2.0 because they predated its impact, but they reflected a cultural shift that has been important to the way Web 2.0 has evolved. A business report published in 2007 by IBM that reprised the title of Sergio Zyman's book clearly cited the impact of changing patterns in consumption and consumer influence on content as major issues for the advertising industry. In its opening paragraph it states:

> The next five years will hold more change for the advertising industry than the previous 50 did. Increasingly empowered consumers, more self-reliant advertisers and ever-evolving technologies are redefining how advertising is sold, created, consumed and tracked... Traditional advertising players –

broadcasters, distributors and advertising agencies – may get squeezed unless they can successfully implement consumer, business model and business design innovation.

A continued decline in the impact of traditional advertising models means that organizations will have to look elsewhere. The future of marketing communications rests with the art of conversation. Engaging in conversations is what public relations people have always done. PR has always operated through intermediaries and persuasion and reasoned argument have always been important elements of what we do.

It seems natural then that in the second iteration of the internet, PR people should join the coders and the designers as the third wave of skilled practitioners required for effective online marketing communications.

Issues management in the new Wild West

Crisis and issues management has always been an important subset of public relations. For some time a good issues management portfolio has included the ability to manage issues in an online environment. We used to think in terms of B2B and B2C: business-to-business and business-to-consumer. Now we have to deal with C2C communications. One of the biggest drivers of consumer-to-consumer communications is dissatisfaction. In Philip Sheldrake's *Social Web Analytics eBook 2008* he states that 'The discontented spread their discontent. The neutral say nothing. The content say nothing. The delighted spread their delight.' I agree with this mantra but what I have observed is that the discontented spread their discontent more vigorously, more effectively and more often than the delighted spread their delight.

There is a trend emerging that I first noticed with consumers who were unhappy following the purchase of big ticket consumer items. In the last 10 years I have worked with two major motor manufacturers and two leading kitchen retailers. One thing that kitchens and cars have in common is that they cost a lot of money. It follows that if you are dissatisfied with your purchase your dissatisfaction is likely to be proportionate to the scale of your outlay.

Traditionally, if you don't get immediate redress through customer service it was customary to take your grievance to the media, usually through a consumer champion. In the United Kingdom, the apogee of media consumer champions is the BBC's *Watchdog* programme. This can present something of a bottleneck for the consumer, given that a very small number of cases make it on air.

Now that consumers can publish their own content they are doing so as a much more viable alternative in applying pressure to an organization than channelling their complaint through an oversubscribed media outlet. Consumers are registering sites or creating blogs as a way of publicly airing their grievances. These sites not only put companies in the spotlight but they attract other disaffected customers. They are also using social media to present their case in more effective ways – for example placing a video of an incomplete kitchen installation on YouTube.

This trend is problematic for companies because of the increasing importance of search in making purchase decisions. According to a survey conducted by Accenture, 67 per cent of UK consumers research products via the internet before shopping in a store (Accenture, 2008) and 70 per cent of online consumers said they use the internet to research everyday grocery products (Prospectiv, 2008). Without doubt these figures will continue to grow.

There are PR techniques for dealing with these situations. Although the techniques are in their infancy we can start to codify some aspects of how to deal with them. In common with a lot of PR 2.0 techniques we start with the approach that we might take when dealing with an ongoing customer issue that was generating negative press coverage in offline media. The one essential difference is that discussions at certain stages of the process will be in public.

Let us consider a situation where a customer believes they have bought a car with a generic engine fault. They start a forum with the name of the make and model in the title and URL. Soon there are a number of discussions taking place that refer to this fault and others. Very quickly there is a site that suggests that the fault may not be isolated and also that a number of car owners are unhappy with the model. The manufacturer has a problem on its hands:

Step 1

We need to identify or at least find a way of making contact with the unhappy customer. This is not as straightforward as contacting a conventional journalist. Some social media sites like YouTube will allow you to send a message to a content supplier. Whatever the site, there is usually a way of getting a message sent and starting a dialogue. In the worst-case scenario you would post to the site and invite the customer (and perhaps others) to contact you.

Step 2

Once you have established contact, the dialogue that follows will feel more familiar. It is important to separate your role from that of customer service; however, you may well act as a go-between between the aggrieved consumer and your client. Your role will be to advise the client what the negative impact on the brand is likely to be in terms of reach and severity. Your role in talking to the customer/forum moderator will be similar to the role you play in talking to consumer champions in conventional media, seeking both to reassure that the problem is being addressed and to make representations with regard to the impact of the coverage.

When you come to advising on the reach and severity of the impact you need to be aware of what tools are available. These will be covered in more detail later in the book but there are many. Alexa rankings, Google Analytics and ranking in search generally will be significant. You also need to monitor general coverage to establish whether the forum is being covered anywhere else or is generating wider interest. Google Alerts provides a useful tool for doing this.

Throughout the process you will need to actively brief the client. You will have to explain the nature of the problem and the particular characteristics of the medium as the conversation unfolds. It is likely that the individuals within the organization that you are representing will have varying levels of understanding of the space.

Step 3

Manage the resolution of the issue from a public relations perspective. You need to make it clear to your client at an early stage that the problem must be resolved satisfactorily. It should, as a minimum, do everything that a fair-minded consumer audience might expect. If it can exceed expectations and can do so in a shorter time frame then its image and its brand will benefit from the positive impression this creates.

Step 4

Decide how to participate in the forum. Participation as a fake happy and satisfied vehicle owner would be a form of astroturfing (see Chapters 4 and 7) and is a complete no-go area. The best route is likely to be the participation of a spokesperson from the manufacturer. They should be open and honest about who they are and clear about what redress is being taken. If they receive critical comments they should be advised to rise above them. This is no place for debate. If a forum member is unfairly critical it is quite likely that other forum members will take them to task. This is a place where the tide can turn with alarming speed. An organization can gain significantly from demonstrating integrity and decisive action in search of a solution even in the potentially hostile environment of a dissatisfied customer forum.

Step 5

Manage the aftermath. Once something exists on the web it can stay there to all intents and purposes forever. You have to negotiate with the originator for a fair and equitable outcome. If you have treated them fairly then they should do the same. You should ask them whether they would consider handing over the domain. At the very least your aim should be for them to shut the site down once they feel it has served its purpose. Alternatively you may recreate it as an open customer service centre.

10 Horses and courses

With all PR campaigns we need to make decisions about the appropriateness of particular media strategies and the relevance of different channels and titles. It is the same when we take our campaigns online. In fact, there are particular vertical sectors that lend themselves to this environment far better than others. The way in which we will approach the social web will vary greatly depending on who we are doing it for.

For example, if you are running a business-to-business campaign for a company manufacturing supplies for, say, the electrical or plumbing industries, engaging with social networking sites is less likely to immediately help you meet your objectives. If, however, you are working in the music industry and you are particularly focusing on a younger audience, then engagement with the social web will be a core part of what you're doing. It is unsurprising that entertainment generally and particularly those areas with a keen interest from the young – music, film and computer and console gaming – integrate best with the social web. Ultimately, every campaign will incorporate some aspect of the social web and every PR person will need to be versed in the tools and techniques of digital communication. When we are evaluating the need for digital public relations we should ask ourselves some questions, as listed in the next section.

Evaluating the need for digital PR

Who are our target audiences?

One of the staggering things about the internet is the sheer richness and volume of information available to you, if you know where to look, and increasingly even if you don't know where to look. By that I mean that the tools of the internet are shaping themselves in such a way that information is starting to come to us rather than us having to find it. Even without using sophisticated data like Target Group Index (TGI) we can discover a lot of things about our target audience and their consumption of online media from a variety of freely available online sources.

If you want to establish a rapport with audience groups that are skewed below the age of 30 then digital media will be an important part of their consumption and they are likely to be active participants on the social web. In early 2007 I took part in a presentation on social media at the UK government's Central Office of Information (COI) with my colleague Charlotte Thompson, then a Managing Partner at McCann Erickson, and Bronwyn Kunhardt, then Head of Corporate Reputation and Diversity at Microsoft UK. I credit Charlotte for introducing me to the idea that the changes taking place in the functioning of the social web reflected changes taking place in society as a whole and vice versa, a subject that I covered in the first chapter of this book. At this presentation Bronwyn talked about the notion of digital natives and digital immigrants. This is a concept popularized by media mogul Rupert Murdoch, who said in a speech to the American Society of Newspaper Editors in 2005:

> Like many of you, I'm a digital immigrant. I wasn't weaned on the web, nor coddled on a computer. Instead, I grew up in a highly centralized world where news and information were tightly controlled by a few proprietors, who deemed to tell us what we could and should know. My two young daughters, on the other hand, will be digital natives... The digital native doesn't send a letter to the editor anymore. She goes online, and starts a blog.

For completeness I should say that Rupert Murdoch was not the originator of this concept. The term 'digital native' was coined by Marc Prensky, an acclaimed speaker, writer, consultant, self-styled futurist, visionary and inventor in education and learning. He used the phrase in 2001 in an article in the academic publication *On The Horizon* to describe a new breed of student going into education with a view of the world born out of a lifelong exposure to the web. Suffice to say that we should converse with digital natives in their language even if it means for many of us that we have to work hard to become fluent.

Are there any characteristics of the web that suit our campaign or sector?

We need to consider if there is something about the way people gather information online that makes it a better place for us to have conversations than conventional environments. I remember a very long time ago being told that eventually video conferencing would completely do away with the need for face-to-face meetings. I now believe, as I suspect most do, that nothing will ever completely replace personal contact.

There are certain characteristics of the internet environment that are particular to it. One very important aspect is that participants can choose if they wish to remain anonymous. It is also an environment where we can conduct research and ask questions without any fear of embarrassment. This is why it is of particular value in the world of health care. Some aspects and concerns about health and well-being can involve a level of personal embarrassment; a good example might be the areas of sexual health and contraception. This level of embarrassment is going to be exacerbated for younger audiences. Organizations should exercise particular caution in this arena because it is unlikely that the web-based communications will be a substitute for personal professional advice. Nevertheless, the opportunity to maintain anonymity is very attractive to many and is a powerful driver in the trend towards seeking information about health online.

Can we give them something?

This is a very important question. With traditional marketing we didn't need to consider very much the inherent value of what we were communicating. There were some exceptions: competition prizes, promotions and offers at the point of sale (buy one get one free or BOGOF in marketing speak — does this hint at some contempt for the consumer?).

When we consider what we can give it doesn't have to be physical, but it could be. For example, if you work in fast-moving consumer goods and wanted to create a Facebook group you could consider giveaways for those that sign up as members. If you operate in the technology sector you could build an online community around your brand and offer them the opportunity to purchase products ahead of them becoming available in retail outlets. These ideas are quite straightforward, using tried and tested techniques.

What the social web provides is the chance to use ideas to give our consumers something new and different. In a celebrated video, *Dove Evolution* (also see Chapter 11), launched online in October 2006, later broadcast on television and in cinemas in some countries, Unilever gave the consumer 'insight' into the tricks of the beauty industry. It is a very short film, just one minute 15 seconds of a normal-looking girl being transformed into an iconic billboard model. It is fast cut and takes the viewer through the expected hair and make-up routine but then takes the image into a digital photoshop style environment. Here the model's neck is lengthened, her eyes and mouth are moved and enlarged, with the final shot appearing on an advertising hoarding with the strapline 'No wonder our perception of beauty is distorted'. This opening of doors, bringing the consumer into the distorted world of fashion and beauty, resulted in the film being viewed by over 10 million people. That kind of audience makes for very powerful communications.

Another major brand that has used the new technologies available to build a community, to engage with its customers in a new and different way and ultimately to give them something extra, is Nike. Nike realized that by just providing a running shoe it was not actually involving itself with the experience of running. Amongst the running cognoscenti Nike wasn't really considered to be a first-choice brand.

For a mass-market brand it needed to find a way of tapping into the actual running experience. It landed on a couple of key pieces of insight. The first was that many people like to listen to music whilst running. The second was that regular runners tend to develop an interest bordering on obsession with times, distances and speed. Nike joined forces with Apple to provide Nike Plus, a system that would work with an iPod nano to provide data about the run. In the words of Trevor Edwards, Vice President of Global Brand and Category Management for Nike, the system:

> combines the physical world with the digital world. We put a sensor in the shoe that speaks to the iPod, and you can hear how far you went, how long you went and how many calories you've burned, pretty simple thoughts. And then, when you dock it, you have a world of information at your fingertips. You get to see all that you've done, all your runs stored in a very simple, intuitive web experience where you can set goals for yourself. You can see how you've progressed. You can actually map your run anywhere you go. In addition, you can join in the Nike Plus community where you can challenge your friends or other community members to run physically, but compete virtually.

Nike used new technology not just to give added value to its users but also to build an online community of over 200,000 members within two years of its launch, based around not just a shared interest but also around a branded product.

Is there a traditional high level of engagement?

If you work in an environment where traditionally there is a high level of engagement between brand or organization and the consumer, then participation in the social web is mandatory. Take the music industry as an example. There has always been a high degree of participation and involvement on the part of the consumer. Fans go to see their favourite artists playing live and they are avid consumers of information about them. Critically in this sector, the way in which the consumer acquires the product has moved quickly into a digital environment, with CDs and other formats displaced by MP3s. A watershed in the relevance of social networks to the music industry was the emergence of Sheffield band Arctic Monkeys, which was attributed to their initial popularity with fans on MySpace.

Another sector where engagement is high is politics. It is my view that the social web will have an enormous impact not just on politics and politicians but in time on our political systems and even on the basic implementation of democratic principles. For the time being it is important to understand that the opportunities for conversations online, and the possibilities for voter participation, are increasingly significant. Political advisers, particularly those involved in communications, have become aware that a digital media strategy is an essential part of the political campaign. For the voter, social networks are already providing tools and applications that allow us to scrutinize our political leaders more closely.

Politics

In the words of Dan Rather, the US veteran TV news anchor, 'Candidates do hate, genuinely hate, audience participation, because they like to control the environment.' When faced with the idea that voters will ask them questions via a YouTube video, he says, 'they get the shivers'.

The long-term effects of using user-generated content and other aspects of the social web on our political systems will be fascinating to observe. There is no walk of life where messages have been more tightly controlled than in the political arena. As brands and corporate bodies begin to learn that they are operating in a world where the customer talks back, politicians will come to learn that they need to do far more than pay lip service to their promises of listening to and respecting the opinions of their electorate.

The level of scrutiny that they will face will continue to increase and there will be greater availability of physical records in terms of audio-visual recordings of what they do and what they say. These records will be searchable and will exist for very long time, making politicians ever more accountable for their promises.

YouTube: it's for us not you

Whilst the political world has been quick to embrace the new channels and opportunities presented they have frequently failed to demonstrate a true understanding of the nature of the new channels. YouTube, for example, is not a new way to watch television (although it can be used for that), it is a platform for democratizing and disseminating video content in a huge variety of forms.

In the summer of 2006 the UK government announced that it would be using YouTube. A Cabinet Office spokesperson said:

> YouTube is just one example of how people are changing the way they communicate all the time. Government needs to keep pace with these changes and ensure we are always looking at new ways to reach people with the things that they need to know. We are open to new ways of communicating, we are watching the digital revolution all the time and developing our own ways in government to communicate.

The government uploaded two short films under the username 'publicservice'. The first was a video explaining 'transformational government' strategy. The second was about Whitehall plans to save money by bringing together service departments. Ian Dunmore, Director of Public Sector Forums, said: 'This looks like the first time a government anywhere has used YouTube in this way. However, we don't expect the videos to surge to the top of the popularity chart just yet.'

For 'not just yet' I think we should read 'not ever'. Two years after posting, the first clip has attracted less that 20,000 views. Another short film, also entitled *Transformational Government — Enabled By Technology* and posted by a user named 'ukgovernment', attracted less than 1,000 viewers in over a year.

For politicians this isn't a channel for sterile broadcasts; it is more often an instrument of scrutiny and there have been some very powerful examples of this already. George Allen was the Governor of Virginia and in August 2006, he was seeking re-election. Whilst on the campaign trail in Breaks, Virginia, he was filmed saying, 'Let's give a welcome to macaca, here. Welcome to America and the real world of Virginia' to a young campaign worker who was working for the Democrat opponent. George Allen was using the word 'macaca' as a racial slur to refer to Shekar Ramanuja Sidarth, an Indian-American, and a supporter of the Democrats. Macaca means 'monkey' and is commonly used in French-speaking African countries like Tunisia – where George Allen's mother grew up. The recorded comment was uploaded to YouTube where it was viewed by hundreds of thousands of people and generated controversy in the wider media. Allen had been expected to win re-election to the governorship of Virginia quite comfortably but he lost by just a few thousand votes. The YouTube video was widely considered to be a major contributing factor. The wider impacts were significant: in part due to this defeat, the Democrats gained control of the Senate, and the course of history was altered in another significant way. According to the *Washington Post*, Allen might have been a contender for president:

> As Virginia voters prepare to go to the polls Tuesday to help choose the Republican nominee for president, state and national party leaders are left wondering: What if former senator George Allen had never uttered the word 'macaca'? After years of preparing for a 2008 presidential run, including trips to Iowa and New Hampshire and formation of a national network of donors, Allen's use of the word on August 11, 2006, changed the landscape of the nominating contest.

The US election of 2008

The United States presidential election of 2008 was the first major democratic process anywhere in the world where the use of social media played a significant part in communications and in all probability in the result. Of the 18 candidates running in the primaries for the two main parties, nine had blogs, including both Hillary Clinton and Barack Obama. Hillary Clinton's campaign staff had an internet director and she used some sophisticated techniques in her campaign for the Democrat nomination like geotargeting her website. IP geocoding makes it possible to identify where a particular PC is geographically situated. Using that technology, Hillary Clinton's team tailored sites for voters in particular states. For example, during the Indiana primary, voters in the state logging onto to her campaign website would have seen the headline 'Help Hillary Win in Indiana', whilst other voters would have seen a generic site.

Tracking the election

The number of US citizens who regularly go online for news about the presidential campaign nearly doubled between 2004 and 2008. According to research released by Pew Research Center for the People & the Press, 24 per cent now turn to the internet, with increased usage of social networks and online video. When you isolate younger age groups the total is even higher with 42 per cent of 18 to 29 year-olds using the web as their main source of information. The most important sources are news sites like MSNBC, CNN and Yahoo! News but young people are also looking at social networks like YouTube and MySpace as well as blogs like the Drudge Report. The survey was conducted 11 months before the election so these figures are likely to have risen considerably.

The internet provided us with far more tools for monitoring and evaluating an election than ever before. Google maps provided an application that allowed us to see exactly where the candidates had been campaigning. You could do this live to see which candidate would be where on any given day or you could track the candidate's performance in terms of the intensity of the campaign trail over any period of the campaign.

Yahoo! News created a 'Political Dashboard' that allowed users to track key political data and issues in a single window. These included poll averages, prediction data from Intrade (an exchange where speculators can trade on political events like politics, producing surprisingly accurate predictions), Yahoo! 'buzz' generated by actual searches and financial, demographic and historical data provided by the Associated Press. MSN provided an Elections '08 Leaderboard and a Candidates and Issues Matrix.

In the previous presidential election we would have turned to the 24-hour rolling news on TV to get the latest information but in 2008 that was not always the case. Web-based sources were often first to the scoop. Political blogger Patrick Ruffini, was the first to announce Obama's surprising victory in the Iowa caucus. His use of Web 2.0 techniques to be first with the news was staggering. In case you don't understand how a caucus works I will briefly explain because of its important to the story. A primary is a traditional secret ballot whilst a caucus is more like a large public meeting. Members of the party gather and hear speeches and engage in discussion before voting for a candidate, and crucially the vote is not secret; it is visible to those at the meeting. In the Iowa Democrat caucuses voters show support for a candidate by standing in a designated area. So if you are at the meeting you can see how the vote is going to go usually at least 30 minutes before it is counted. Before the Iowa caucuses, Patrick Ruffini used Facebook and his own blog to recruit caucus goers and then he got them to sign up to Twitter. He asked them to tweet the results from inside various caucus sites to a special Twitter feed that he had set up for the purpose. Although there are 1,784 precincts in Iowa, each with their own caucus, the 70+ Twitter feeds and the scale of Obama's lead allowed Ruffini to predict the result at 7.20 pm Central Time, well before the caucuses closed and ahead of all of the national and local news organizations. 'Twitter is revolutionizing newsgathering and real citizen journalism. The crowd will know about it before the media knows about it,' Ruffini said later.

All sorts of tools were available to the general public like 'Complete Election Coverage 2008' from Compete.com, which included lots of tools for analysing the performance of the candidates' websites through to buzz measurement. Google Trends also provided a powerful way of evaluating the level of public interest in each of the candidates as the various stages of the election progressed.

Campaigning via social networks

Involvement in social networks was significant from the earliest days of the primaries. Republican Mitt Romney was the first prospective candidate to launch a Facebook profile, Democrat John Edwards set up a campaign headquarters in the cyberworld of Second Life, which resulted in one of the more unusual Web 2.0 occurrences when it was vandalized by the avatars of his political opponents. Hillary Clinton used her website to launch her campaign. Barack Obama was a prime mover from the outset. He actively engaged with most of the high-profile social networking sites, including MySpace, Facebook, Flickr, YouTube, LinkedIn, Eventful and Twitter. He was also able to promote his campaign through the social network exclusively aimed at African-Americans, BlackPlanet.com, a community with over 20 million members.

The 2008 presidential campaign showed increasing convergence between old media and new social media. NBC News and msnbc.com joined up with MySpace to create the Decision '08 site to be part of MySpace's political channel Impact. It featured video clips coverage and blogs from several NBC news broadcasters, including Brian Williams, anchor of *NBC Nightly News.* The site also linked directly to the MySpace pages of the candidates, Obama's being the more polished of the two, with at times as many as 10 times the number of friends that McCain had.

Another link-up provided a new take on the presidential debate whilst delivering a PR coup for YouTube. A link-up with CNN meant that for the first time, US presidential candidates faced questions directly from voters via video clips. In a sense this was a major change, with the traditional role of the political journalist making way for the voice of the electorate.

Larry Sabato, Director of the Center for Politics at the University of Virginia, said: 'This will become part of the process in at least some debates in all future primary and general elections. It's an innovation and it involved the public and especially young people, and that's all to the good.' He did point out, however, that the public lacks the skills and depth of knowledge to test politicians in the way that journalists can.

Interaction with social networks was very much a two-way process in the run-up to the election. On the day that Barack Obama announced he was forming a presidential exploratory committee in January 2007, student government coordinator, Farouk Olu Aregbe, created a group on Facebook called 'One Million Strong for Barack'. In the spring of 2008, when it was clear that Obama would win the Democrat nomination, a group was formed on Facebook called 'Stop Barack Obama (One Million Strong and Growing)'. By the summer of 2008 this group hit the 1 million total whilst the original and much older pro-Obama group still had only 600,000 members. There was also an anti-Hillary Clinton campaign on Facebook: 'Stop Hillary Clinton (One Million Strong AGAINST Hillary)', which took just 10 months to gain 1 million members.

UGC and voter power

There is little doubt in my mind that the ability of the ordinary person to post and publish on the internet, will in time have a significant effect on the balance of power between the politician and the body politic. The evidence to support that argument was clear in this election. Oh Boy Obama! was an unofficial site produced by supporters of the Democrat nominee described as an 'online think tank' where people voted on policy ideas that they believed Barack Obama should adopt as part of his campaign. Oh Boy Obama! was a Digg-style site that showed how political ideas could be tested against real grassroots opinion with those most likely to succeed in winning popular support rising to the top.

Funding

The social web was critical to the Obama campaign in another quite fundamental way. Right from the outset it played an important part in the funding of his bid for presidential office. In a campaign video directed at his supporters he said, 'Instead of forcing us to rely on millions from Washington lobbyists and special interest PACs [political action committees], you've fuelled this campaign with donations of $5, $10, $20, whatever you can afford, and because you did, we've built a grassroots movement of over 1.5 million Americans.'

The *New York Times* reported that Senator Obama 'raised $95 million in February and March alone, most of it, as his aides noted... in small contributions raised on the internet. More than 90 per cent of the campaign's contributions were for $100 or less, said Robert Gibbs, the communications director to Mr Obama.' Obama's success raising money via these small donations was achieved in a way never before possible as part of a US presidential election campaign.

Entertainment

The arrival of the social web has utterly transformed the entertainment industry. It has had a crushing effect on huge sectors of the entertainment industry and in particular the music business. In its annual survey of senior executives in the media and entertainment industry, in 2007 Accenture reported that the media and entertainment businesses feared that user-generated content was a major threat to their industry. 'Traditional, established content providers will have to adapt and develop new business and monetization models in order to keep revenue streams flowing. The key to success will be identifying new forms of content that can complement their traditional strengths,' said Gavin Mann, digital media lead for Accenture's Media and Entertainment practice.

Returning to the earlier questions about the appropriateness of social media to the sector, we can see why it so relevant. The audience for the entertainment industry and particularly the music industry is very much skewed towards the young. I also posed the question as to whether there are any characteristics of the web that suit our campaign or sector. This is clearly self-evident when it comes to the entertainment industry. As soon as internet speeds allowed it, the transfer of music grew at such phenomenal pace that it very quickly became the preferred method. Whilst the music industry chose at first to stand in the way of a tidal wave of popular demand, the sheer market forces at play changed the industry. With even faster internet speeds available a similar revolution is under way with film and television.

Given that the internet is now home to such a high volume of entertainment it is essential that anyone involved in any way in the promotion of the entertainment industry should be immersed in the social web and well versed in the communications techniques of digital PR.

Multi-platform is the new multi-channel

Multi-channel is a term that has been employed for some time in both the media and the marketing industries. In television it was the term used to herald the arrival of a multiplicity of choice available through cable and satellite. Multi-channel marketing is the use of different media channels to reach an audience in a variety of ways and in different situations and at different points in their daily life.

Now, in addition to multiple channels we have multiple platforms available. These platforms are defined by content and by technical devices. In terms of content, platforms might include television, radio and web-based platforms including websites and social networks. Device-specific platforms would include mobile TV and applications designed for things like the BlackBerry, iPhones and a multitude of other mobile devices.

Increasingly, the entertainment industry is conceiving ideas that will operate across many of these different platforms. In January 2008, BBC Three, the digital 'youth' channel, relaunched itself as a multiplatform channel brand. One aspect of this involved broadcasting on the internet as well as through conventional TV transmission. Another aspect has been to promote user-generated content through its website.

Public relations activity needs to keep pace with the media and also with the organizations that it promotes. PR people working within the entertainment industry need to consider opportunities for delivering their campaigns over multiple platforms as well as through multiple channels.

Industry and commerce

Those areas of business where the relationship with social media is least obvious are those that have been most resistant to the idea of engaging with their consumers in this way. For the traditional marketeer it is entirely counterintuitive to promote your product or company in an environment that you do not manage. Many senior marketeers, particularly those controlling large advertising budgets, have always had some difficulty with the world of public relations because they do not control the ultimate output of the PR campaign. The fact that the end result is ultimately what a journalist writes rather than a piece of advertising on which they have final sign-off has always been something that they felt slightly uncomfortable with. These individuals are generally only persuaded of the value of PR because it can lead to endorsements that have a value that can only come from an independent third party — the balancing counterpoint to the ceding of control.

It is totally unsurprising that these same people feel quite uncomfortable in the world of conversations where the voice of consumers will usually be louder than their own. The issue here is not whether you should participate but how and where and when you should participate.

The reversal of influence

Business organizations like many other of society's structures have to come to terms with the changes brought about by the ability of their customers to talk to one another and to influence each other's purchase decisions. Previously, the main form of interaction was a monologue delivered by a business to its consumers. Now there are many dialogues. Many of these, as I have indicated previously, are consumer to consumer, and their impact is far greater than the monologues that preceded them. Some of these dialogues are between businesses and customers and these discussions will replace many of the old ways of marketing and PR. Brands are going to become an expression of these conversations.

The power of brands will become more closely aligned with the real value that they bring and the actual difference that they make to people's lives. The consumer or rather an aggregation of your consumers will become the brand innovator. Instead of companies telling people what to buy, people will tell companies what to make.

Fortune favours the brave

'In the long history of humankind those who learned to collaborate and improvise most effectively have prevailed.' These are not the words of some emerging Web 2.0 guru but those of Charles Darwin. Another of his observations was that 'it's not the strong that survive, it's not the intelligent that survive, it's the people that respond to change'. Those organizations that understand that the world has changed, that realize that they must also adapt to a new set of rules and that have the courage to participate in a space that they no longer control will be the ones that prevail.

This is not an easy change for many organizations to make. The hierarchical structure of many businesses is designed to manage and control outcomes. Whilst marketing has always been regarded as something of a maverick element it remains a managed process.

Many businesses simply aren't geared up to adapt and to respond to change.

Dell was one of the companies that suffered most from the emergence of citizen journalism. The impact of the opinions of Jeff Jarvis in his BuzzMachine blog (see Chapter 2 for the full story) was widely felt within the organization and it is quite probable that it played a significant part in the decline of the value of the company's stocks. Having suffered so badly in the user-generated content environment we might have expected the organization to retreat from engagement and to shore itself up against the possibility of future negative public scrutiny. That would have been a very 20th-century response and perhaps we should not be surprised that Dell, having felt the negative effects of Web 2.0, should understand better than most the importance of positively engaging itself with its customers through the new channels available.

Dell created a blog in 2006 called Direct2Dell that subsequently added its own Twitter feed. The company then hit upon the idea that Twitter could be used as a way of marketing surplus stock. The Dell Outlet was launched on the micro-blogging service, offering Twitter-only promotions. In addition to making offers available in an incredibly quick and direct way, Dell was also connecting with a group of highly influential opinion-formers who are likely to influence other less technical potential customers.

Dell's Twitter strategy revolved around posting special offers with tweets containing a time-limited offer. Ricardo Guerrero, who led the development of the strategy, was persuaded of the value of Twitter in a *New York Times* article that suggested that it gave users a kind of social sixth sense. Dell Outlet's Twitter also linked to Dell's Direct2Dell blog. In less than a year the Twitter account generated $0.5 million worth of business for Dell.

Twitter has another aspect to it that can alter the way a corporation is viewed. Twitter is incredibly personal. When individuals interact with a company via Twitter, they are dealing with a real person. This can have a very beneficial humanizing effect on the way a corporation is perceived. Michael Brito, the founder of the blog site Conversationsmatter, summed it up:

I follow guys on Twitter like @RichardatDELL. He is a real person that I can have a real conversation with. He is not Dell Corporation nor is he hiding behind the Dell logo. He is a human being and I can relate to him far better than I can a corporate entity. And, since I have been following Richard, my relationship with Dell has evolved. When I look at the Dell logo on my laptop or walk by a Dell Kiosk in the mall, it's much more personal.

All Dell blogs and social media properties feed into Twitter and @Direct2Dell is the co-ordinating account. Not every Dell Twitter has an individual identified behind it as some are just corporate: @DellDirekte, @Alienware and @DellShares. By clicking on any of the Dell Twitters being followed by @Direct2Dell, you can see the individual Twitter account of the person behind that account. Dell has over 50 individual Twitter feeds.

Dell also created a Digg-style site called IdeasStorm, which was designed to give users the opportunity to contribute ideas and then comment and vote on them as a way of improving Dell computers and customer service and support. As a direct result, based on the votes of 120,000 users, Dell produced a laptop that comes installed with Linux rather that Windows.

Another major corporate to use Digg-style voting is Starbucks. The launch of My Starbucks Idea in March 2008 was intended to make Starbucks the 'most deeply connected brand in the world', said Chief Technology Officer, Chris Bruzzo. Any visitor can look at the ideas that have been posted and read the list of ideas that have been taken up by Starbucks in the 'Ideas in Action' section. Registered members can submit ideas, or vote and comment on ideas submitted by others. Starbucks has also created a dedicated team of around 50 'Idea Partners' who are all Starbucks employees, chosen because of their level of expertise in areas that range from coffee to community programmes. Their role is to monitor the site and present the best and most popular ideas to senior decision makers. Members votes are worth 10 points and each idea's score is displayed on the site.

Within weeks of the launch of the site, Starbucks launched a product called Vivanno, which it attributed to the demands of users for healthier options, with more real fruit, fibre and protein.

Vivanno drinks contain no artificial colours, sweeteners or high fructose syrups. At the launch in the United States two flavours were available: Orange Mango Banana Blend and Banana Chocolate Blend. The launch was announced on the site by 'Katie' or 'Sbx_kt', a 'My Starbucks Idea' partner and registered dietitian and senior nutritionist employed by Starbucks:

> You've asked for options that give you energy and deliver real nutrition to support a healthy lifestyle, while also tasting great and with moderate calories. Today, I'm personally very proud and excited to introduce Vivanno™ Nourishing Blends – a solution to your quest for Healthier, High Protein options and the first of many new items to come.

Another major corporate to leap into the social web is the US car manufacture Chrysler. The motor industry is facing a particular challenge with a number of marques having to deal with blogs and forums created by unhappy owners. Chrysler has taken the proactive approach with the Jeep brand and created the Jeep Community.

The Jeep Community has a home page that unites a broad range of social media sites where they have seeded content about the brand, the main ones being Flickr, YouTube, Facebook and MySpace. The site also has a share function that explains how to connect and share your experiences with Jeep, allowing the site to embed content from followers on Flickr and YouTube.

This is an incredibly smart move. In an arena where people are posting their experiences, good and bad, the Jeep Community drives interest, traffic and more important links to all of the positive 'on brand' coverage. This means that all of this favourable content will rank higher when a prospective Jeep customer types the brand name into Google.

The Jeep Community points visitors to other groups, so users can participate in discussions. The site pulls in news and lists events – even providing a calendar function to allow the diehard Jeep enthusiast to plan their life around the brand. There is a 'legacy' section that provides information on the history of the Jeep and there is even a section called Jeep Swag. Earlier in the chapter I talked about the idea of giving something to the consumer as being an important driver of social media engagement. Jeep Swag does exactly that. There are free games and downloads as well as the opportunity to buy merchandise that allows you to live the brand – including a Jeep kayak and a branded baby buggy. The community links directly to the Jeep Facebook and MySpace sites that include branded pages and content of their own, with videos and pictures.

11 Digital PR architecture

I started lecturing on PR and the internet in 1994. I was invited to do so by Dr Daniel Moss (or Danny as he has always introduced himself), Principal Lecturer and Programme Leader for the MA in Public Relations at Manchester Metropolitan University. In those days the content was merely theoretical, as the world wide web barely existed, access speeds were very slow and there were few tools available. Around that time I would speculate about the possibility of sending images to journalists by e-mail. This was technically possible then but impractical and most journalists didn't have e-mail addresses anyway.

I had an e-mail address at the time, which although not exactly memorable was, I recall, 100342.2451@compuserve.com. Because having an e-mail address was slightly unusual I was asked by Tony Murray, the then editor of the marketing title *Adline*, to write an article on the subject of e-mail for the May 1995 edition of the magazine. When I was researching this book I discovered the article on an old 3.5-inch floppy disk and it makes for amusing reading now:

> Everyone's talking about it, everyone's writing about it, the age of E-mail has arrived!... no it hasn't. At the moment for the vast majority, E-mail, the Internet and the Information Superhighway are just another confusing set of expressions with less direct relevance to them than the Soviet Space Programme.

E-mail. The very description is jargon and therein lies E-mail's greatest problem. Until people understand that sending E-mail is as easy as using the telephone and probably easier than using the fax, it won't take off.

So how do I know that the age of E-mail hasn't arrived? Well, we've had E-mail at Pro-Action for the best part of a year and it just isn't used that much. Our E-mail address is printed on our letterhead, in our brochure, on all of the press releases we send out and even on a 'cyberspace' directory accessible by over three million people, but almost nobody ever sends us any E-mail. I monitored our messages over a few weeks and for every piece of E-mail we received, we had sixty items of normal mail (so called 'snail mail'), thirty faxes and over eighty phone calls.

We've used E-mail to send messages to let me see… about six people; a TV trade publication in Amsterdam, my brother who's an accountant who's not sure exactly how to send E-mail back to me, my friend Adrian who is a heart surgeon, *Adline*, Granada TV's computer show *The Program* and Stephen Fry. They've all replied apart from one… *Adline*.

So what is E-mail? Well, you type a message into your computer, click with the mouse to send it via a 'phone line and that's it. Next time the recipient logs on to their system they can get the message, easy. You can now get text readers that deliver the messages in a human voice. If you have the right kit you can send a message using your own voice… if you could just send a message instantly with your own voice you would have, wait for it, a telephone!

So is E-mail a waste of time? Emphatically no. At the moment it is a bit like having one of the first fax machines. The quality is a bit dodgy and no one else seems to have one. In ten years time if you don't have E-mail your business won't be taken seriously. For the PR industry in particular E-mail will change the way we work. You will send a press release for approval and get it back maybe minutes later. It can then be sent directly into the computers of all of your target publications, in seconds. You will even be able to attach a high quality photograph in a format ready for the paper or magazine to drop straight onto a page. All this without leaving your desk. Better still you could do it all from a gite in the South of France because unlike a fax or phone your E-mail address number is portable, it goes with you. It will revolutionize the industry, but not yet.

I note that text readers haven't really taken off and I still don't have a gite in the South of France.

Much has changed since those days and the way that we conduct the practice of public relations has evolved considerably. However, there is no doubt that we are at something of a juncture, albeit one that the people will pass through at different times and at different speeds.

Digital PR, ePR, PR 2.0 or the New PR, it doesn't matter what we call it, does signify a change. It means changing what we do and how we do it. It also means that we will have to structure our PR programmes in new ways.

Sometime in 2006 when I was discussing some of the issues surrounding Web 2.0 with my work colleagues in the digital arm of our company I wondered whether anyone had consider using the term PR 2.0. I did a search and discovered that of course they had. In doing so I came across a blog by Stuart Bruce, one of the United Kingdom's leading practitioners and early adopters of the use of social media and social networks. His blog 'A PR Guy's Musings' has been going since 2003. When I searched on the term PR 2.0, I alighted on a posting on Stuart's blog entitled 'Big PR firm falls for the PR 2.0 hype'. In his opening to the piece he states the following:

> For some time I've been talking to clients and potential clients about PR 2.0. It's a good way for a small-technology PR consultancy like BMA PR to differentiate itself and attract attention. However, after getting noticed I then always point out what a stupid idea PR 2.0 is. This whole PR 2.0 or 'New PR' is such a pile of garbage. What I'm doing is simply an evolution of what I've always done.

He finishes with the line, 'We might have to have different conversations with different people using different channels but that is simply the evolution of our profession. It's not PR 2.0'.

I have referenced this blog in a number of lectures that I have given over the last couple of years. I think Stuart's principal point that we are engaged in an evolution of what we've always done is right but I believe that there is more to it than that. It might be semantics (more of that later) but I believe that some things have changed and many things need to be done differently. According to Wikipedia, a 'revolution (from the Latin *revolutio*, "a turnaround") is a fundamental change in power or organizational structures that takes place in a relatively short period of time'. I don't think that's a bad description of what's happening. The terms evolution and revolution are often used as if they were mutually antagonistic. I don't think they have to be. I think that some aspects of PR are evolving at the same time as some fundamental shifts are taking place in organizational structures.

I believe that digital PR campaigns will have quite different architectures from their conventional antecedents. Predominantly, the structures of traditional PR campaigns have been quite linear. We begin with some observations and background, we move on to defining our aims and objectives, we define a strategy, identify our target audience, agree the tactics and delivery and then evaluate the results. The most important phase, the delivery, is also often quite sequential. This might be determined by the lead times of the media that we are targeting during the campaign. For example, if we were launching a major new product we might have embargoed conversations with consumer magazines several months before we reveal the new product to trade publications and shorter lead time titles. Then finally, perhaps a couple of weeks after we brief the trade press, when the launch is imminent, we stage manage a major reveal for national newspapers and broadcast media.

Digital PR campaigns will be much less linear. We will find ourselves managing campaigns in which research, delivery and evaluation are all being conducted simultaneously.

The same... but different

To elaborate on the theme of concurrent evolution and revolution, public relations is the same in some regards as it was before and in many is quite different. Can we approach blogger engagement in the same way that we approach media relations? Blogging is not the same as journalism, although many journalists also blog. One of the principal differences is that there are no editors and no publishers to moderate or interpret the content, or to maintain any level of quality control. There is a quality control mechanism that does operate and that is popularity. Great blogs, and there are many of them, are both popular and highly influential. I believe that the way we approach these bloggers should be very similar to the way in which we approach good journalists, that is, with a strong idea or a piece of useful insight or information. You probably wouldn't send either of them a press release. That is not to say that press releases are never useful but I tend to agree with a former colleague who believed that the press release should come at the end of the conversation not at the start.

Does the internet merely add another dimension to our channel strategy? As I indicated earlier I don't regard the internet as just another media channel. You could look at it as a sort of parallel universe of media channels. This universe is so vast and complex that we won't be using all of it all the time. Online PR campaigns should be built up using a variety of the different online channels in a way that is suited to the communications challenge at hand. This echoes the process of media selection, which has always been a part of the business of planning a PR campaign.

As part of the planning of a digital PR campaign you should decide which elements of the social web would be the most suitable and build ideas around how you harness those elements in delivering your programme. This is perhaps more easily said than done and there are a great many potential pitfalls. I believe that the aspects of the social web are so diverse that in time PR people will start to specialize in particular areas; for example, developing expertise in the dynamics of WebTV and video with a particularly detailed understanding of YouTube, or having a specialized understanding of social network sites like Facebook.

The critical thing is to understand what you're doing. Because this is a new and emerging discipline there is huge temptation to develop your offer too quickly. The bold assumption that engaging with the social web simply means developing the techniques of traditional public relations might encourage practitioners to believe that they need nothing more than their existing skills and experience. The agency PR market is highly competitive and the ability to offer a specialized digital PR service provides a competitive edge. Don't be tempted to offer advice too early. Learn from the mistakes of others, immerse yourself in the world of the user-generated content and educate yourself before you attempt to advise others.

Embracing complexity

The level of complexity that we now face seems at first to be incredibly daunting. If we go back not much more than a decade it seemed that the media was entirely quantifiable. Every good PR person could name every national daily and Sunday newspaper and probably had a pretty good understanding of the editorial stance and range of content for most of them. Within less than a year of entering the public relations profession most account executives would be able to name the regional newspaper for every single town and city in the United Kingdom. To this day, whenever I hear the name Arbroath, the word *Herald* pops into my head.

Now we are dealing with a communications architecture that is far more complicated to map out. It also adapts and morphs at an alarming speed. There are new digital channels appearing all the time, with others disappearing or declining in importance. These changes are impossible to keep pace with in the way that we kept pace with changes in traditional media. We need to accept that these channels are in a permanent state of flux and we must constantly seek out new intelligence and information.

One example of the increasing complexity is the notion of 'distributed conversations'. Essentially, these are discussions that start in one place on the web and then continue elsewhere, perhaps in a multitude of other places, not as separate conversations but as fragmentations of the original discussion. For example, a discussion might begin with a blog post and then continue on FriendFeed. Discussions will often go off in different directions if they occur in different places.

Whilst the internet becomes more complex and it becomes harder for us to seek out that which might be of interest, more and more tools and applications are being introduced to help the information find us. Changes in search, the increasing simplicity and greater ubiquity of RSS (Really Simple Syndication – see Chapter 4), combined with the evolution of social bookmarking (Chapter 4) helps us to separate the wheat from the chaff.

Link building — the new cross-promotion

For 20 years or more, the marketing industry has been obsessed with the idea of integration. The nature of the internet is such that if we don't integrate, our online communications may forever languish in some digital backwater.

The idea of a link or hyperlink is central to the concept of the world wide web. If we want to increase traffic to our online content then we need to find ways of creating links that will take people to it. You need to understand how links work and build linking strategies into your digital PR programmes. You can if you choose, work with specialists in this area, but if budgets don't allow it there are some basics that you can learn and should implement.

Unless you have used a search engine, following a link is one of the most common ways to find new content on the web. A link suggests authority not just in the Technorati sense (see Chapter 3) but in the literal sense. If a site you trust offers to lead you somewhere for more information you are more likely to have a look. Link building is about quantity, but for this reason it is also clearly about quality. Links also elevate your Google rankings. Search engines give sites with good genuine links a higher ranking.

In many senses the social web is about community and by having links to other places you are playing your part in the community. Effective and appropriate linking can make you part of a powerful network.

To maximize your links you must operate strategically. First, you must have the quality of content that other sites might wish to link to. You should also have clear and relevant outbound links from your site. The most persuasive argument for other sites to link to yours is that you have already linked to theirs. You should also build a list of target sites from which to request links, preferably ones that you have already linked to. You must approach them in a way that is personal and that allows you to be clearly identifiable. Approaches that look in any way automated will be ignored. The use of software in locating sites that you might choose to link to is acceptable and makes a good deal of sense. Using software to make your actual approaches to the sites is both unacceptable and largely a waste of time.

Reciprocal linking works well but not all sites are of equal value. It stands to reason that if you can engineer a reciprocal link from a site that ranks highly on Google that will deliver more than a link from a site that doesn't. An effective link-building strategy involves generating links that will drive traffic. By picking a few good sites, e-mailing them individually with details of exactly what you can offer and where you think a link might fit in with their existing content, you will not only get a greater response rate, but the links you get are sure to be far more valuable.

You should avoid working with companies that offer to create multiple false links; these are known as link farms and this is a form of 'black hat' search engine optimization (see Chapter 5). Not only is this unethical but it is one of the best ways to get Google to eliminate your site or relevant content from their databases altogether.

Finally, do not treat the social web as if it exists in isolation. One of the best ways of building interest in your content and persuading people to link their content to yours is to have conversations and interaction in the real world. Issue press releases about your content and send them to offline as well as online media. Talk to as many people as you can about what you are doing. Send links to interested parties in an e-mail – make sure they are likely to be interested, don't spam them. If you can engage with users do so and encourage them to spread the word.

Memes

As digital PR specialists we will be asked by clients to assist them with online viral marketing. It is a mistake to enter into a campaign with viral marketing as the central feature. That is not to say it is impossible to deliver, but it is exceptionally difficult. To imply that a piece of content such as an image or a video clip will achieve viral status at the outset of a campaign is a bit like guaranteeing that the campaign will be of national award-winning quality before you have even come up with the ideas.

In any case, I prefer the idea of internet memes to the 'viral' concept. It is a better description and it carries more explanation, which gives us a better chance of providing clients with a clear understanding and managing expectations, if you endeavour to create something 'viral'. In addition, the viral concept is generally understood to be propagated through e-mail whereas a meme may spread using a variety of interconnections.

Meme is one of those words that is more often seen in print than spoken out loud, and as such is often mispronounced. So, before we go any further I should tell you that it is meme to rhyme with beam and not me-me.

Richard Dawkins, the author of *The God Delusion* (2006), originally came up with the term in a book published in the mid-1970s called *The Selfish Gene*. It was coined to describe how Darwinian principles could explain the spread of ideas and cultural phenomena like fashion, music, catchphrases, architectural styles and even beliefs. Dawkins argued that memes propagate themselves in societies in a way that is similar to the behaviour of a gene or virus. The meme is a cultural unit or idea that spreads rapidly. The term has gained greater currency with the growth of the internet. It appears that the world wide web is particularly suited to the propagation of memes and so we now have the concept of the internet meme.

An internet meme is a cultural unit – often a video, an image or a story that spreads rapidly across the internet, passed mainly from person to person. It is the propagation of a file or even just a hyperlink through e-mail, instant messaging, blogs and social networks. The content is usually based around humour, rumour or insight. A meme might be a parody and some memes inspire parodies that also become memes – for example, the *Dove Evolution* video described in Chapter 10 was a meme that inspired *Slob Evolution*, another meme. In a way a meme is a genuine expression of pop culture.

There have been examples of internet memes where people have inadvertently become famous through the memetic spread of a video clip. Examples of this include Star Wars Kid and Tay Zonday with his song *Chocolate Rain*.

YouTube has played a key role in the spread of great number of memes. The 'Rickrolling' phenomenon is an excellent example. Rick Astley was a UK popstar who had number one hits on both sides of the Atlantic in the 1980s (full disclosure... and showing off: I had the pleasure of working with Rick Astley in a PR capacity at the start of his singing career). His still catchy hit *Never Gonna Give You Up* went to number one throughout Europe and in Australia in 1987 and hit number one on the Billboard Hot 100 in the United States on 12 March 1988. Rickrolling was a prank that originated on the image board site 4chan in which a link to somewhere (such as a specific picture or news item) would instead lead to a video of Rick performing *Never Gonna Give You Up*. The first instance of a Rickroll claimed to be a link to the first trailer for *Grand Theft Auto IV* but instead it took you to Rick. The prank quickly spread across the web. Because most of the links were to YouTube it quickly became aware of the phenomenon and on 1 April 2008 as an April Fool joke the website Rickrolled everybody who clicked on one of their front-page featured videos. There are several Rickroll links on YouTube that have had a combined total of over 30 million hits.

Not far behind Rick Astley in the video meme stakes is Matt Harding with a combined total of views on YouTube of over 20 million for his 'WherethehellisMatt' videos. Matt is from Connecticut and in his thirties. He was a computer games developer who quit his job in February 2003 to go travelling. Several months into a trip through Asia a travel companion gave Matt the idea of performing a peculiar dance, apparently the only dance Matt does, on the streets of Hanoi. The video was posted online and attracted some attention. Harding repeated the dance in a number of locations and edited together 15 scenes of this dance with the background music *Sweet Lullaby (Nature's Dancing Mix)*, by Deep Forest, which uses lyrics from a dying Solomon Islands language. It attracted the attention of Cadbury, which was launching a new chewing gum range called Stride. Cadbury offered to pay Matt to do another trip around the world to make a new video. In 2006, Matt took a six-month trip through 39 countries on all seven continents, dancing in all of them. The resulting video gained more coverage and resulted in Matt getting e-mails from all over the world. In 2007 Matt went to Stride with the idea of travelling around the world one more time and inviting the people who had contacted him to come and dance in his videos. His third dancing video resulting from this trip was released on 20 June 2008. The video was the result of a 14-month journey to 42 countries.

This time the video used a piece of music called *Praan* composed by Garry Schyman, with lyrics adapted from the poem 'Stream of Life' from *Gitanjali* by Rabindranath Tagore.

The Stride sponsorship is probably one of the best ever examples of marketing involvement in an internet meme. It worked so well because it was done in a very empathetic way. The company took a risk and paid for Matt's travel. There was no guarantee that they were going to get what they wanted. The branding on the video is also incredibly subtle, limited to a short end frame. The 2008 video with its choice of music and the participation of so many different people from around the world is actually a very moving piece of film. I would hazard a guess that the marketing people involved with the Stride sponsorship had some input into the edit. Whether that was the case or not the end result was very sympathetic to the spirit of the original film.

It is probable that a variety of factors combine to create memes – some are manageable but many are not and therefore it is foolhardy ever to promise the delivery of 'viral content'. Some PR campaigns are more likely than others to result in a memetic spread. I believe that for this to work a number of factors have to coincide. These factors are incredibly difficult to quantify or pin down but might include some of the following. There should be some genuine quirkiness contained within the idea. The meme could coincide with some kind of zeitgeist or spirit of the age. Humour is a powerful component. Often it will contain an aspect that challenges conventional wisdom. There is also a critical mass factor at play. The spread of an idea or concept will accelerate at some point probably due to the multiplier effect of people being exposed to it more than once. This might be described as a bandwagon effect.

Whilst the internet is particularly suited to the spread of memes, this kind of effect was observed before the internet. Fashion and music are areas where this is common and there are also crazes like the Rubik's Cube, the mechanical puzzle invented in 1974 but which exploded in popularity during a few months in early 1980, eventually selling over 300 million units.

Whilst we cannot promise to deliver memes as part of a PR campaign we should be able to recognize them and to facilitate their development. The arrival of Punk Rock in the 1970s was partly memetic but it was also the result of Malcolm McLaren's innate understanding of the media and his ability to manage the provision of strong themed stories surrounding the Sex Pistols.

The Wikipedia entry on internet memes specifically references their relevance to advertising and PR:

> Public relations, advertising, and marketing professionals have embraced Internet memes as a form of viral marketing to create marketing 'buzz' for their product or service. Internet memes are seen as cost-effective, and because of their (sometimes self-conscious) faddishness, a way to create an image of cleverness or trendiness. Marketers, for example, use internet memes to create interest in films that would otherwise not generate positive publicity among critics. The film *Snakes On A Plane* generated much publicity from this method. Political operatives use internet memes to shape opinion. Used in the context of public relations, the term would be more of an advertising buzzword than a proper internet meme, although there is still an implication that the interest in the content is for purposes of trivia, ephemera, or frivolity rather than straightforward advertising and news.

Semantics

Semantics is the science of meaning. For communicators, meaning is important at every level and semantics has always been significant (the Greek word *semantikos* means significant) in how we craft the language of our written communication. As a term, semantics has taken on additional meaning when it comes to the web.

The semantic web, usually encompassed in the idea of a third-generation web or Web 3.0, is the vision of Tim Berners-Lee, the creator of the world wide web and is an evolution of the web in which the semantics or meaning of information is defined to a common standard. This vision would make the information on the web infinitely more searchable and discoverable. At the core of this is the Resource Description Framework (RDF), a way of describing web content. You might recall (Chapter 4) that the original RSS feeds were RDF Site Summaries and there is a relationship between the idea behind RSS and the semantic web. The current version of RSS is a simplification of the original, containing less information. The redesign of the web to semantic standards would make the discovery of information more intuitive.

In May 2006, Tim Berners-Lee said, 'People keep asking what Web 3.0 is. I think maybe when you've got an overlay of scalable vector graphics, everything rippling and folding and looking misty, on Web 2.0 and access to a semantic Web integrated across a huge space of data, you'll have access to an unbelievable data resource.'

Web 3.0 and PR 3.0

Those that dislike the term Web 2.0 tend to detest the idea of Web 3.0 even more and they are both artificial constructs. The sheer volume of data on the web may prevent a semantic web from ever coming to fruition. The infrastructure may never grow sufficiently well to support it. Concerns over access to personal data and issues of privacy may get in the way of its development.

If Web 3.0 may never come to pass, treat with extreme caution anyone that raises the notion of PR 3.0. An article in the US edition of *PRWeek* in April 2007 entitled 'Industry Enters a New Age: PR 3.0' was met with a deluge of criticism from bloggers.

12 Tools of the trade

Any new discipline will require new techniques and new tools with which to implement it. As PR people we have always supplied content in the form of written words, images and on occasion both audio and video. This will continue to be something that we do. We have always sought to engage with influential opinion-formers to seek to persuade and influence the content that they produce. We will continue to do this too.

We will also continue to do this using most of the methods that we already have at our disposal. Face-to-face briefings will continue, we will still spend a lot of time on the telephone and we will carry on using our skills to craft the written word. Despite the growing outcry about the volume of poorly targeted e-mails that clog the in-boxes of information-overloaded journalists, we will still be using e-mail. We will also need some tools that have been designed to meet the needs of a different age and that have been adapted to suit the ways of the social web.

The Social Media Release

The Social Media Release (SMR), sometimes referred to as the Social Media News Release or Social Media Press Release, is becoming talked about more and more as an adjunct to or even a replacement for that mainstay of public relations, the humble press release. In short, the SMR is a press release that is posted on the web, and done so in such a way that will improve the likelihood of content being disseminated.

History of the SMR

Tom Foremski joined the *Financial Times* in 1999 to help expand its US technology coverage and analysis. He became their US Technology Correspondent and a regular columnist. In May 2004 he became probably the first journalist from a leading newspaper to resign and become a full-time blogger, despite the fact that he had a highly influential job in journalism and had never blogged before. He created a blog site called SiliconValleyWatcher, an online business news magazine focused on the industry in Silicon Valley. Within three months of starting and without any kind of full-scale launch, it was named by Bacon's, a leading US media-tracking group, as one of the most influential in the United States.

On 27 February 2006 he posted a blog entitled 'Die! Press release! Die! Die! Die!'. It opened with the line 'I've been telling the PR industry for some time now that things cannot go along as they are... business as usual while mainstream media goes to hell in a hand basket'. He went on to describe the press release as nearly useless and destined 'to reach the digital and physical trash bins of tens of thousands of journalists. This madness has to end. It is wasted time and effort by hundreds of thousands of professionals'. As an aside, Tom has another social media claim to fame as he was the person that outed the YouTube diarist LonelyGirl15 as a fraud.

What happened next was quite extraordinary. The response to Tom's post from within the PR community was immediate. One agency in particular decided to rise to the challenge. A PR company with offices in Boston and San Francisco responded to the article with a concept for a new form of press release. Just three days after the blog post, SHIFT Communications created what was the probably first SMR, albeit in a prototype format. It appeared on Todd Defren's PR Squared blog. Todd, who is Principal at SHIFT Communications, opened his post with the line 'Okay, Tom, how is this for the press release of tomorrow?' in direct response to Foremski's article. The release was to announce the launch of a robot dinosaur named Pleo from a company called UGOBE. It contained lots of links, was light on spin and contained assets like financial data, tags to other stories, options for photographs and both executive and analyst quotes, most of the things that Tom Foremski had asked for in his piece. It also contained links to videos. Tom approved and immediately posted the following: 'the always resourceful Julie Crabill, from SHIFT Communications on Tuesday sent over what she called a "Foremski-style" news release, and the same release old style. And it is a good example and a great step in the right direction — just these simple things already made the news release a lot more useful'.

In May, Edelman entered the ring with its take on the SMR. Edelman CEO, Richard Edelman, made a keynote speech to an audience at the 2006 Syndicate Conference in New York City, a B2B conference focused on emerging trends and technologies in content syndication. He announced that Edelman would be releasing a 'physical manifestation' of the reinvention of the press release in June. 'It's better to say, "We're going to give you a set of info with tags and you organize it as you wish." We'd rather have it in pieces as if it's a b-roll [supplemental footage] and let bloggers make the news judgement.'

SHIFT Communications beat Edelman to the tape and created the template for the first Social Media News Release (SMNR) and announced it three months after Tom Foremski posted his diatribe against the press release. Todd Defren announced it on his blog PR Squared and made it clear again that it had been a direct response to Foremski's post:

> This newfangled press release format has been baking since late February, thanks to the rantings of Tom Foremski at Silicon Valley Watcher. The template was and is 100 per cent open and available to anyone who wanted to use it. It didn't look great but the content was comprehensive. It went further than Tom Foremski requested in terms of content and it also had built in syndication links.

Edelman wasn't quite as quick in releasing its version of the SMR as it had hoped. The June deadline came and went and it was December before it announced the release of StoryCrafter, a 'web-based software tool for helping companies produce and deploy social media news releases'. The format had been tested by Auburn University, and Robert French of the university's Department of Communication and Journalism said:

> StoryCrafter provides a simple, yet complete, format and process for the creation of social media releases. For those new to the process, using StoryCrafter helps you understand the formatting and layout, too. And, the StoryCrafter tool offers all of the options called for in the Social Media Club's list of key elements for a social media release.

There is some debate as to whether an SMR should allow comments to be posted directly into it. My view is that they should not. The SMR is an instrument for disseminating information to social media using the conventions of Web 2.0 but I don't believe that it should act as a social medium in its own right. This is at best a distraction from its main purpose. The danger is that given the novelty of the form, the SMR can become the subject of discussion rather than the news content of the release. A very good example is the Edelman announcement of StoryCrafter (although uniquely in this particular case I accept that the content of the SMR and the news were virtually one and the same). Perhaps rather unfairly a lot of the comments were criticisms of Edelman rather than of the StoryCrafter SMR itself. Here's just one: "'I don't know anyone at SHIFT Communications, and I've never met anyone there, but this is a blatant rip off of their Web 2.0 press release", Posted by Russell Page, Thursday, December 07, 2006 at 2:42:30 AM'. Another critical difference in the approaches taken by the two companies SHIFT Communications and Edelman was that Edelman's version of the SMR was not openly available and was designed for its clients only.

Various other versions of the SMR have been developed since, like Shannon Whitley's PRX format based on the SHIFT SMNR template. PRX is an XML format, which, like Todd Defren's original template, is an open standard, freely available to anyone that wants to use it.

Another significant player in the emergence of the SMR is Chris Heuer, co-founder of the Social Media Club, an organization for people interested in creating and consuming Web 2.0 media, referred to in Richard Edelman's speech announcing the launch of StoryCrafter. The Social Media Club was created for the purpose of sharing best practices and establishing ethics and standards in social media marketing, as well as promoting social media literacy. A central project of the Social Media Club has been to develop the hRelease, an alternative SMR standard.

In February 2008 the International Association of Business Communicators (IABC) took on a leadership role in the development of the SMR. The IABC announced that it would coordinate the effort to develop standards for the SMR, combining flexible formatting options with a common tagging standard. The stated goal is to make business news usable by online reporters and bloggers, as well as more discoverable in search engines. The journalist who started the whole thing, Tom Foremski, commented, 'It is great to see all the work that has gone into transforming the news release into something that reflects the use of the many new media technologies that we use every day.'

SMRs: what they are and how they work

Whilst I have covered various standards and iterations for SMRs there are common aspects that make them different from press releases posted on the web. It is important to note that the SMR has its own presence on the web. It isn't something that you e-mail to a journalist or blogger. It is something that they discover or are invited to view.

SMRs will be enabled for social media links to bookmarking networks, tags for search and links to other relevant content. An SMR will contain searchable content including tags that allow interested parties to discover the release. It will also be shared through social bookmarking and RSS. An SMR might also include multimedia content like audio or video clips.

Brian Solis, one of the leading commentators on PR 2.0, summarized the content of an SMR and I have largely followed his summation of a standard SMR template:

● headline;
● intro paragraph, including keywords;
● supporting facts;

- selection of quotes;
- multimedia – audio, video and images;
- RSS — company and/or product news;
- link to insert in social networks (Facebook, Bebo, MySpace, hi5 or others);
- blog this (link to blogger platforms);
- share on Twitter, Jaiku, Pownce or Tumblr;
- other bookmarks;
- other relevant links;
- links to news aggregators and communities including Digg and reddit;
- further information details and links could include an image plus vCard, or links to LinkedIn, Facebook or Twitter feeds.

The SMR is still very much in a period of evolution. There are those that question the validity of an SMR or even whether they are needed at all for a digital media relations programme. My belief is that they will get better but they still offer some considerable advantages over the traditional press release. You don't have to send out a copy-heavy e-mail, you can just send a link. They are tangible in that they exist on the web in their own right and are discoverable. They also solve some of the problems of choice that the old press release threw up. Because of the problems of file sizes (and before that cost) we tended not send out too many images. Now we can offer a choice that might include the company logo, a head shot of the chief executive, a picture of a product or the event that the press release covers and possibly also a really creative picture that we might have considered too risky to send before because it would only be suitable for certain types of publication.

Social Media Newsroom

Your Social Media Newsroom is where you will publish your SMR. It's not the only place where you can do this but it is the most elegant solution. The Social Media Newsroom is an evolution of the digital press office or pressroom that has been around for years, often as part of a corporate website. The original digital pressroom acted in many ways like a press release archive.

SHIFT Communications, architects of the first SMR, claimed to have developed the first ever Social Media Newsroom on its website, created in conjunction with Shannon Whitley, founder of PRX Builder. This claim, I think, is more difficult to substantiate given that the Social Media Newsroom is an evolutionary idea.

The Social Media Newsroom contains many of the features of a traditional online newsroom. It allows all of a company's relevant audiences to access a variety of content from press releases to reports and images. It will probably contain information on senior management including images and biographies. It would contain a press release archive and a photo library. There might also be a corporate diary with dates for key announcements and key events.

In addition to all of these traditional web assets the Social Media Newsroom would have a number of interactive features. The contact section for reaching press officers and key spokespersons might include Skype numbers, IM (instant messaging) links or Twitter feeds, as well as the more traditional contact details. The newsroom should contain links to press coverage with one-click opportunities to e-mail these or share them with aggregators, social bookmarks or blog trackers like Technorati. There would be a multimedia library in addition to the conventional photo library. The press releases would be SMRs. Plus, there would be a section with a choice of RSS feeds and a section for links to social bookmarks. The Social Media Newsroom should also provide for direct conversations about individual news releases, actually on the company site.

Creative digital assets

As PR people, our ability to work collaboratively with people with different skills will have a significant impact on the scale of the projects that we can advise on and play an active role in the development of. Whilst the opportunity for creating digital assets has been hugely democratized, creativity in photography, audio and video production and design are not our core skills. We must engage with creative people from other disciplines, particularly those who have made their mark in web design and functionality in order to be able to deliver the most powerful digital PR campaigns.

Take, for example, a couple of Web 2.0 initiatives from two of the world's motor manufacturing giants. One of these I have referred to in Chapter 10. Chrysler's Jeep Community is, I believe, a tour de force in the field of social media marketing. The visible benefits are clear: it is a place where the real Jeep enthusiast can go, to discover a rich vein of content, to interact with other enthusiasts or to start a journey through other social media networks. There are also some other less immediately obvious benefits. The Jeep Community site is designed to be content-rich and to change frequently. It is regularly updated and it manages significant numbers of both in and outbound links. All of which will lead to a high Google page ranking and will help to raise the rank of all sorts of other positive content about Jeeps. In an era when all car manufacturers are facing the challenge of disaffected and disgruntled owners posting comments and even starting blogs and forums to published articles detailing their grievances and inviting those of others, finding a way to elevate positive content is a powerful strategy.

The second initiative that I want to draw your attention to is the GM Europe Social Media Newsroom. It's a good newsroom, it is very clean-looking and it contains links to a great deal of rich content through sites like YouTube and Flickr.

Both of these are digital PR initiatives but neither could have been achieved by PR companies acting alone. They required coders and designers, particularly in the case of the Jeep site, which has a really powerful look and strong design aesthetic.

13 Evaluation and measurement

The internet provides us with a huge range of ever more complex tools for measuring our online marketing activity. We can target our audience far more effectively than ever before, we can identify and direct communications to the 'long tail' (see Chapter 4) and we can feed back market intelligence into our campaigns in a cycle of constant improvement. Having said all this, a cohesive system of evaluation and measurement of online PR programmes remains the 'holy grail' of social media marketing and digital public relations. Lots of people are seeking the answer; we know that when we truly find it, it will be incredibly valuable and there are a myriad of false claims of discovery.

To some extent that's where the analogy ends because there are a significant number of tools already in existence that allow us to monitor and measure activity on the web in general and measure some of the direct impacts of our activity. The amazing thing about these tools is that they not only provide in-depth analysis but they are also in the majority of cases entirely free to use. The issue for most public relations practitioners operating in this arena is that there is no single tool or dashboard that provides us with a one-stop solution. Any kind of social media audit or in-depth analysis of what is going on is therefore fairly labour-intensive at present.

Now that we are well into the 21st century there is a proliferation of communications technology that might be influenced by PR discussions in chatrooms, forums, blogs, social networks and newsfeeds. The way we consume media has changed irrevocably and it has been multi-layered, with one channel interwoven with another. Business-to-consumer (B2C) monologues have been supplemented by B2C2B dialogues and customer-to-customer (C2C) discussions.

When measuring the impact of digital public relations and its effect on activity within the social web and we find ourselves overwhelmed by the scale of the task and the range and complexity of the data, we should keep one thing in mind from PR's analogue past. In practice, the industry has never allowed itself to get too caught up in the detail of measurement and evaluation. I don't mean that we don't consider it to be important or are not able to do it accurately, but simply that detailed and in-depth analysis has a time and a place.

The measurement of key message delivery, pre- and post-campaign quantitative and qualitative research and measurement against benchmark data are all available to us and are used in some campaigns. More often both agencies and their clients as well as in-house departments are content to use fairly simple and straightforward media evaluation techniques such as the measurement of combined circulation figures for media coverage or the advertising value equivalent. Our experience often allows us to judge the success or otherwise of a campaign by using a combination of these simple evaluation techniques combined with our instincts and judgement.

It is inevitable that we will approach social media measurement and analytics in a similar way. This chapter aims to give you an idea of the sheer range and diversity of the measurement techniques at our disposal; how and when you decide to use them is entirely up to you and in practice we are likely to pick and choose different tools for different campaigns.

Fortunately, a number of companies, including many of those already producing distribution, media monitoring and evaluation services to the PR industry, are developing products in this area. It is tempting to try and do the in-depth evaluation ourselves because so many of the tools are free. It is my belief that detailed analysis has never been a core skill of the public relations professional and it makes sense to outsource it. As well as describing some of the free tools, this chapter will identify and explain some of the products and services offered by third parties.

Almost all the evaluation and monitoring techniques are automated and use algorithms. In fact, if they weren't they would be completely impossible to use in any meaningful way with the scale of the data out there. This does present us with some serious challenges. I had been using Meltwater News, the Norwegian-based online news monitoring service, to provide a daily feed of online news coverage across a range of clients. The system allows you to operate with a range of 'search agents' that you can modify to search news sites with a collection of terms that you have specified. One of the clients I was monitoring was UPS or United Parcel Service Inc., the global express carrier and package delivery company. One of the key search terms was clearly going to be the company name UPS. Unfortunately for non-case-sensitive searches (and in the company logo lower case letters are used) the initials UPS are identical to the word 'ups'. Initially we were seeing a lot of information about 'business start-ups', quite a lot about fuel prices hikes or rather 'top ups' and a fair amount about 'pin ups'.

Search ranking as evaluation

There is a fairly persuasive argument that the single most important objective of most PR programmes should be to impact on the search ranking. It is fairly simple to benchmark a campaign in this way by conducting identical Google searches pre- and post-campaign and this, notwithstanding the impact of other activity or other marketing campaigns running simultaneously, should provide us with a critical measure of the influence we have achieved. This method for evaluating PR effectiveness is also very closely aligned with most organizations' business objectives.

In fact, we could regard Google page ranks as a proxy for brand influence and the difference that occurs over a period of time will give us a strong indication of brand momentum. Search engines alone are designed to spider the totality of the web so only a search engine can measure the cumulative effect of coverage across the internet.

Online tools

If you intend to do your own social media measurement and evaluation then there is a vast and ever-increasing array of tools available. Most of these deliver a level of functionality at no cost. This means that you are free to experiment with them and discover their individual strengths and limitations without incurring any costs other than the cost of committing your time to the project. You must bear in mind that although they will improve over time many of these tools are quite flaky and don't always give you the results you want or expect. By using a number of them in conjunction with each other you are more likely to get robust results.

Google Alerts

Google isn't just the leading search engine; it has in recent years been acquiring and building additional applications and devices that allow users to monitor and measure what is going on the web in a variety of ways. Google Alerts are e-mail updates of the latest relevant Google results based on your individual choice of topic – which could, for example, be the name of a client or product. The uses of Google Alerts include monitoring news stories and keeping tabs on developments. The system allows you to identify what type of Google search data you want to keep abreast of; for example, you could elect just to search either blogs or news or you could request comprehensive alerts. You can also choose how to get the alerts, weekly, daily or as they happen. Because it is free to use you could also use Google Alerts to provide you with current information on a competitor and on broader industry issues.

Google Trends

Google Trends is a phenomenally powerful tool that allows you to monitor activity on virtually any subject or organization that interests you. You are able to monitor up to five topics simultaneously and see how often they've been searched on Google over a defined period of time. You can choose to show results over a specified time frame or region. When you specify results for a specific year or multi-year period, each point on the graph shows a week's worth of searches. When you restrict the results to cover a single month, each point on the graph shows a day of searches. You can also drill down into geographical regions and compare different search levels in different territories with information that is updated daily.

Google Trends analyses web searches for the item you enter, compares them to the total number of searches done on Google and then displays these in a graph. Below the search volume index graph is a news volume graph that shows you the number of times the search topic appeared news stories. For many searches there will be a spike in news coverage and when this happens Google Trends detects it and shows the headline from a Google News story that coincided with the peak in news coverage so you can see immediately what was happening to cause this increase in interest.

You can also use Google Trends to spot hot topics of interest by following 'Hot Trends'. Hot Trends, which is updated hourly, shows the internet's fastest-rising searches, which can give you a picture of the major issues and interests at a point in time. You don't have to do this just for the day that you are searching. You can go back over a substantial time period (currently over a year) and discover what the fastest-rising searches were and what the search activity looked like over the course of any particular day.

Google Analytics

Google acquired Urchin On Demand, a powerful set of web analytics tools, in April 2005. It combined the service with other related tools to launch Google Analytics, a free service that generates detailed statistics about visitors to websites. It is a tool for tracking your own website or blog rather than a general tracking tool and you have to embed the tracking code into your site. The code is supplied and can be cut and pasted. Blog hosting sites like WordPress make this incredibly easy by providing a box for you to cut and paste the code into.

Google Analytics can track where visitors are coming from, whether the hits are generated by search engines, by referrals from other sites (and what sites these are) or from advertising, pay-per-click networks or e-mail marketing campaigns. It allows you to determine exactly what is driving visits to a site, which will in turn help you refine your digital PR efforts and how you integrate it with other elements of digital marketing.

Google Analytics has an easy-to-follow high-quality dashboard with graphical representations of much of the data including graphs, pie charts and highlighted maps that show exactly where traffic to the website is geographically coming from. As you drill down through the dashboard there is a very rich supply of in-depth data that allows you to identify where visitors come from and how long they stay. The system also has highly sophisticated tools that analyse any e-commerce activity on the site.

Technorati

Technorati (its name suggests the technical literati), is a blog search tool and service that monitors and measure the scale of influence of different blogs. Because bloggers frequently link to and comment on other blogs, Technorati is able track those links and index them, which means that the site monitors communities and conversations more or less as they happen. According to Technorati, there are over 175,000 new blogs created every day and bloggers update their blogs with over 1.6 million posts per day, which translates as over 18 updates a second. The site claims to track over 112 million blogs and over 250 million pieces of tagged social media.

By tracking links between blogs, Technorati has championed the idea of internet authority with the bigger the number of links the greater the authority. Technorati lists its own Top 100 blogs with the most authority (see Chapter 3).

IceRocket

IceRocket incorporates BlogTracker, which will count your blog visits and other blog statistics. Like Google Analytics it is free, but it offers far less depth than GA. The main IceRocket page also identifies major trends and includes a tag cloud of popular current searches.

BlogPulse

BlogPulse is supplied by Nielsen BuzzMetrics, part of Nielson and a significant player in the measurement of user-generated media. BlogPulse provides a number of related tools. The Trend Search allows you to create graphs that show the level of blog coverage or 'buzz' about specific search terms – you can select these so they could be issues, brands, companies or individuals. You can compare up to three search terms. There are limits to the time periods and you can only choose to look at four different time periods: a month, two months, three months or six months. Featured Trends allows you, in a similar way to Google Hot Trends, to spot topics and subjects that people are talking about most in blogs, and to show these on a graph. Conversation Tracker creates a threaded view of conversations that arise from blogs. You can use Conservation Tracker to monitor distributed conversations. When a blogger publishes a post and other bloggers link to it, from those links other links arise, but the conversation may be spread over a range of locations. The BlogPulse Conversation Tracker is a tool for assembling these distributed comments, which it does by performing a traversal of the conversation starting from the original post and following each node. At present, given the data-heavy nature of this type of search, the depth of the search tree is set to three and the default breadth is set to 25 although it can be adjusted.

BlogPulse's Profiles help you obtain in-depth information about specific blogs and their authors. Profiles is based on the information bloggers provide, their linking activity and their posting behaviour.

News readers

News readers have been around so long that for some people they have become an intrinsic way of getting their news. The news reader sits on your computer, ideally on your desktop as a gadget or built into your Windows sidebar so you can see the feed all the time if you need to. They have become infinitely more adaptable over time and many allow you to adapt and manage the content using RSS feeds (see Chapter 4) so that you get exactly the kind of news that you want.

Twitter

Twitter, the micro-blogging site is increasingly becoming highly effective as a way of disseminating news. It works like a personal newswire. The responses on Twitter to events like earthquakes are well documented. The value of Twitter in these situations is that it is instant and unfiltered. News isn't checked but multiple responses, and that is what happens when multiple users experience a major event, combine to confirm the veracity of a story. When a moderate earthquake struck near Los Angeles in summer 2008 official news began to emerge about the quake after just four minutes. That sounds pretty quick until you examine what happened on Twitter. The first Twitter update from Los Angeles said simply 'Earthquake' and it was posted seconds after the earthquake began. At the four-minute mark the word earthquake was trending on Twitter Search with several thousand updates. A lot of news channels get their information from newswire services like the Associated Press (AP) and their news story follows AP bulletins. It was nine minutes before AP announced 'Strong quake shakes Southern California'.

It isn't just earthquakes that demonstrate the speed of news delivered via Twitter. When NASA's Phoenix Mars Lander found water on Mars there were Twitter discussions as to whether the story was true several hours before any major news organization announced the story. This speculation was fuelled by a Twitter feed called MarsPhoenix, clearly written by a NASA project insider as if it were the voice of the lander itself. It twittered the following statement hours before NASA issued a press announcement on the subject: 'An ice-containing sample made it into the TEGA oven. I can now say I'm the first mission to Mars to touch and then *taste* the water. FTW!'

Many news organizations operate Twitter feeds as a way of attracting people to their websites to read news stories in more depth. The *New York Times*, BBC and the *Guardian* are amongst those I follow and in many cases Twitter is where I see the news first. For news organizations and bloggers, the 140 characters is enough to give a real taster of a new story, with room for a URL. One of the really clever aspects of Twitter is that if your URL is long and takes you over the 140 character limit it is automatically converted into a tinyurl. As a consequence, many of the micro-blogs on Twitter point their readers to a web page elsewhere for richer content like images or video or just for more detailed information.

Twitter Search

Originally called Summize, Twitter Search was created by an independent group of software engineers and later acquired by Twitter. It allows you to follow all current feeds on Twitter by keyword. It effectively allows you to operate outside of your own Twitter account and cherry pick from the Twitter universe. As a social media monitoring tool it is anecdotal but also incredibly useful. It allows you to discover and follow emerging trends in real time. It can also act as a fast-tracking mechanism for any type of news story. Simply put in the search term or two, the name of a brand you are working with for example, and you will be able to see immediately who is microblogging about it and what they are saying. There is a really powerful added dimension to this form of social media monitoring. You are not only able to see the individual who created the post but you can contact them directly by sending them a direct message (DM) on Twitter with a single click directly from the page. If, for example, you recognize a particularly influential individual, not only have you discovered that they have an interest in the subject that you are monitoring but you will be able to send them further information personally.

Twit(url)y

Twit(url)y is one of a number of Twitter-related tools that scans Twitter for data. This one searches for the URLs of links that people are twittering about the most. These are grouped into subjects and then ranked on the Twi(url)y home page. This creates a Digg-style ranking of what are the current hot topics. This is a really current news source, with the ability to link straight through to the topics under discussion.

Alexa

Alexa is another website that allows you to track the performance of a website over time. The great advantage over Google Analytics, for example, is that you that you can track any website not just your own. The search and browse feature provides thumbnail images of sites and site information balloons. Alexa site information includes statistics, traffic information and related links pages. If the site you are looking for has an Alexa rank of more than 100,000 the site will display a graph of performance over a defined period of a week, a month, three months, six months or the maximum period for which Alexa has tracking data.

Alexa users can download a toolbar that gives them information on every site that they visit with a single click. The toolbar is integral to the Alexa as traffic rankings are based on the usage patterns of users (combined with data collected from other sources). The Alexa sites ranking is based on a combination reach, determined by the number of Alexa users who visit a site on one day and page views. To a certain extent we could view the Alexa toolbar users as being similar to the panels used for measuring TV and radio audiences. Because this is a sample there is some doubt as to whether this panel is a typical representation of internet users. Does the fact that it is a self-selecting and probably web-savvy sample of the internet user population affect the rankings? It may be that Alexa factors this into its calculations but that isn't clear from the site.

Delicious

The delicious site (formerly del.icio.us) is a social bookmarking website. It stores and shares your bookmarks on the web, instead of inside your browser. This allows you to access your bookmarks from any computer. It also means that your bookmarks can be shared. This allows delicious to rank the sites that people are bookmarking, rather than giving a ranking of what people are visiting like BlogPulse or Alexa. Essentially that means that it provides a rank of what people are interested in.

The other core feature of delicious is that it allows users to tag websites. Tags are single-word descriptions that you add to your bookmarks on delicious. You can have as many tags as you like on a bookmark. Tagging can be easier and more flexible than filing information in folders as it allows the information to be cross-referenced. It also means that you can look at groups of sites sharing a common tag.

Digg

Digg is designed to allow people to both discover and share web content. Users submit links and vote on them. The voting is either positive or negative; digging and burying. This means that the most popular stories and sites appear on the front page.

Users collectively determine the importance of the content, be it news, podcasts, videos or images. This creates a multiplier effect, known as the digg effect, which can greatly inflate traffic for the most engaging and interesting web content.

Socialmeter

Socialmeter is a very simple yet quite useful little site. Paste in a URL for any website and it produces an immediate score based on the number of ratings it finds at nine different sites: Google, delicious, Digg, reddit, Furl, Spurl, Sphere, Technorati and Yahoo!. It's quick and dirty. And it aggregates content, which is one way of evening out the accuracy issues that all of the measurements have.

Quantcast

Quantcast is an open internet ratings service that enables users to view audience reports for sites. Publishers can segment audiences by tagging their websites, videos or widgets. Quantcast seeks to report the audience breakdown that marketeers look for, including traffic, demographics and even lifestyle. Like Alexa, Quantcast ranks sites but unlike Alexa it does not use a tool bar but instead uses embedded code installed in participating websites in a way that is closer to how Google Analytics operates. A lot of Quantcast's data is based on inference: comparing information received from a variety of website publishers. Quantcast can make these inferences because it can log the user's IP address and information via cookies that are placed in the user's browser.

Compete

Compete currently provides information solely for US-based sites. Its analysis is based on a diverse sample of over 2 million US-based internet users who have given their permission to Compete.com to allow it to analyse the web pages that they visit. Compete also sends surveys to the panel to get greater depth. The site uses a number of different tools. Compete Site Analytics provides free information for every single site on the internet. It includes traffic history and competitive analytics for online retailers. Compete Search Analytics is designed to help search engine optimization (SEO – see Chapter 5) activity. It can be used to find keywords driving traffic to a variety of sites, and it allows web publishers to track their performance against competitors. Compete Ranked Lists provides lists of the most popular sites. Compete Tools is a collection of tools designed for use on the desktop with web browsers. It works with both Internet Explorer and Firefox, and provides a snapshot of Compete Site Analytics information as you browse.

BuzzMonitor

The BuzzMonitor was developed by the World Bank, the organization providing financial and technical assistance to developing countries. The World Bank is a global institution and needed to listen to online conversations in multiple languages, across multiple platforms. It was unable to find a solution that would aggregate all this content, make sense of it and allow it to collaborate, so it decided to build its own. It made it freely available and it is a useful tool for communities and organizations interested in tracking videos, photos, blogs and podcasts that cover a specific issue. The BuzzMonitor looks at the source URL and groups all mentions under this URL, so regardless of which feed brought the mention, you see all the mentions from one blog on one page. Each source displays two widgets: the Alexa Link and Rank Button and the Technorati Authority widget. Users can vote on mentions and the votes are published on two pages:

most voted on and most recently voted on. Users can assign tags and in a similar way to delicious, tags can be combined across users. The BuzzMonitor also includes graphs. There are two type of graphs: a trendline showing the number of mentions for a site or by tag and a bar chart showing what the hot tags for the day are. The BuzzMonitor is RSS-enabled, offering feeds for tags and keywords you search on. It also provides tag clouds of what is discussed today, in the past seven days, last 30 days and past six months.

Socialmedian

Socialmedian is a social news network. The site is designed to enable you to keep up to date on the news that you are most interested in. Users of socialmedian can create 'news networks' on any subject that they like. A news network allows a group of people with similar interests to track, share and discuss aggregated news content on a specific topic. Every user gets a personalized newsfeed on their socialmedian homepage. Users can share RSS feeds or submit content by e-mail, or directly via the site. Users identify stories that are of particular interest and can choose to follow other users as their 'newsmakers'. This means that if you identify users who are regularly pulling in news that interests you, you can use them almost in the way that you might follow a specific news channel.

Outsourcing

Public relations organizations have always outsourced monitoring and evaluation and I can see absolutely no reason why they should not continue to do so when operating on the web. Because so many of the tools previously described are entirely free or have free elements, the temptation is there to manage all of the evaluation ourselves. Theoretically, those of us working in agency PR can charge monitoring and evaluation costs back to a client, and increase our revenue. I think that generally speaking this would be a mistake. I think there is every reason for us to use these tools for some sense checking and some quick and dirty evaluation, but I think for bigger campaigns, for which accurate evaluation is an essential part of the delivery, we should seriously consider bringing in outside help and expertise in the way that we have always done, and concentrate on our core skills as communicators. The array of suppliers is dazzling and growing all the time. There is an issue here in that a great number of organizations have seen the commercial potential of providing effective measurement of social media and have rushed to market with untested products and services. The observations below will give you some help in finding a supplier that provides what you require but there is no substitute for direct experience – either by trailing the services yourself or by discussing them in detail with someone who has. The services that they provide generally include some or all of the following with proprietary names and features:

Dashboard

These are usually web-based computer dashboards showing information in real time about your company or brand. This will include graphs and images that will cover things like engagement scores and 'share of buzz' versus major competitors. Some organizations do their own indexing and some draw down data from some of the free sources already outlined is this chapter. Many use a combination of these sources.

Depth reporting

Most of the companies will offer research-based in-depth analysis of social media metrics for a company or brand. This might take the form of a one-off in-depth analysis; alternatively, some providers offer regular, for example, monthly, reports prepared by their researchers and analysts. Here are some of the key players in providing social media measurement services:

Attentio

Attentio is a market intelligence company based in Brussels. The company offers a service called Brand Dashboard, which is used to monitor blogs and other social media to provide insight into consumer behaviour and attitudes. The company also supplies a Buzz Report for companies that want a deeper understanding of how they and their brands, products or services brands are perceived by online consumers.

BuzzLogic

BuzzLogic launched in April 2007 to help advertisers, marketeers and communications professionals improve their online advertising performance, blogger relations and product promotion campaigns. The company offers a piece of proprietary software called BuzzLogic Enterprise. This is designed to enable marketeers to identify key online influencers' blogs and social networks, and to use this information to engage with these opinion leaders. The software generates social maps that visually illustrate the level of influence of participants within an online conversation. The software depicts the connections around key content and individuals.

Cision

Cision is a company with a long history of supplying services to the PR industry. The business has evolved from a press cuttings bureau into a global operator with divisions in 12 countries. The business began in 1892, as part of the Swedish national telegram company Svenska Telegrambyrån. The company, which provided a press cuttings service for Swedish businesses, became known as Pressurklipp. In the 1990s the company began to offer simple media analysis services. In 1999 the company acquired UK-based market leader in press monitoring, the Romeike Group, making it the world's largest media monitoring business. This was followed by acquiring Bacon's in the United States in 2001. The companies were rebranded and relaunched under the Cision banner in 2007. The company offers what it calls dynamic web monitoring, which consists of three components. The first is 'Core Web Monitoring', which uses searches to sites that include the Technorati Top 100, AdAge Power 150, top 100s from the *Times* and *Guardian* and Ogilvy top sector blogs. This, it claims, ensures that you cover the mainstream web. The second component is what Cision calls 'Bespoke Web Monitoring'. Cision works with clients to identify key non-mainstream sites that are directly relevant to them and that complement coverage achieved through its core web monitoring. Finally, when new, influential sites emerge they are added to the monitoring program and those that lose influence are downgraded or eventually removed altogether.

Collective Intellect

Collective Intellect is a social media analytics company that also uses its own intellectual property to search and categorize conversations online as well as identifying key influencers across all social media. Developed originally for the financial services industry, Collective Intellect provides data on social media to more than 60 hedge funds. Collective Intellect indexes internet data, topic by topic, and uses filters to identify and report on influence, sentiment and popularity.

Dow Jones Factiva

Dow Jones Factiva provides business news sources that include the *Wall Street Journal,* the *Financial Times,* Dow Jones and Reuters newswires and the Associated Press. A web platform provides access to this content. Dow Jones Insight provides media analysis. It allows you to monitor public opinion, and benchmark against competitors through share-of-voice analysis of traditional print and broadcast media combined with web content, including user-generated blogs and message boards. Historical data allows you to benchmark past media coverage and look at how your share of voice performs over time. The Media Lab Services provides monthly or quarterly customized reports. Dow Jones Insight has a web-based interface with user-customizable dashboards, which allow you to create custom charts and graphs. The data can be exported to Word and PowerPoint.

Market Sentinel

Market Sentinel was founded in September 2004 and now operates in the United Kingdom, Europe and United States. The business isn't solely about social web measurement and evaluation, its services also stray into the territory of providing PR services targeted at the online environment. It divides its offering into suites. The first of these is Campaign Manager. This is a general market evaluation service that researches consumer and mainstream media to identify trends and provide insight into the themes that a marketing campaign might tap into: the existing conversations around a brand and its competitors and what people are saying about relevant products and services. This informs clients as to how they should tailor their key messages according to changing market conditions.

The second offering is Market Sentinel's Reputation Manager. This is an evaluation of reputation, taking account of any trends on the internet that may affect customers and partners. The service evaluates both reputation and those individuals or organizations that are impacting on reputation. The analysis covers the people talking about you and your brands, their influence and authority, who they engage with and who influences them.

Product Launcher is fairly self-explanatory but again orientated to web conversations and where the level of authority lies for particular market sectors. Post-launch, it offers reports on the reaction and builds in adjustments to the campaign based on the findings. Crisis Manager is Market Sentinel's crisis management service that is designed to monitor the rapidly changing online conversations around a business in a crisis situation.

LiveBuzz is Market Sentinel's proprietary dashboard offer, which provides updates and commentary on brand coverage and key issues in real time on your desktop. The LiveBuzz Dashboard doesn't need prior software installation. Weekly brand performance reports can be generated by the LiveBuzz tool or regular reports drawing on the main themes and key competitive issues are offered and are prepared by the research team. Stakeholder Analysis is the benchmarking suite and tracks authority in relation to brands or issues identifying how others achieve authority and allowing businesses to target resources at influencing them. The Net Promoters Index measures consumer sentiment and tracks these results over time.

Millward Brown

In 30 years Millward Brown has become one of the world's leading research companies, with offices in more than 43 countries. The core services are market research and brand consultancy. The offerings cover communications audits and media evaluation, to brand performance monitoring and measuring the accountability of marketing campaigns. Millward Brown aims to provide research-based advice to help you successfully manage your brand and optimize the return on your media and communications investments. Across the group of companies it has a number of specialist companies including Millward Brown Optimor, a brand valuation business, Millward Brown Precis, a PR service company providing media content measurement and analysis, Global Media Practice, which measures media effectiveness, and Dynamic Logic, which measures online advertising and marketing effectiveness.

Like most of the organizations we have covered in this chapter, Millward Brown offers a selection of proprietary tools. The first of these is BrandDynamics, which aims to uncover a brand's strengths and weaknesses and potential for future growth. ChannelConnect examines the relationship between brands, communication channels and consumers and helps to determine the best communications channels. Dynamic Tracking monitors brand marketing and com-munications performance. Link examines executions: podcasts, banners, TV ads, or any other form of communication and provides guidance on how to improve their performance. TGI (Target Group Index) is the industry standard in pulling together global research to provide consumer insights for over 50 countries.

Through Millward Brown Precis the company offers 'word-of-mouth' measurement. It uses its own TGI data to identify and profile potential transmitters within a category. For example, people who are likely to convince others about purchasing decisions for televisions or audio equipment are also likely to be heavy users of iPods and Sky+. From the information available through TGI it builds a profile of the most effective 'transmitters'. Using Link, Millward Brown claims to determine the 'conversational value' of any proposed marketing activity. Precis also tracks online conversations, through 20,000 online news sources, in excess of 8 million blogs and over 100,000 message boards, forums and Usenet news groups. Reporting and analysis comes through an interactive graphic portal or via written reports.

Metrica

Metrica is a media analysis and evaluation company established in 1993. In partnership with an online news aggregator, Metrica offers online press monitoring and a rolling newsfeed. It offers to track blogs and social networking sites for clients as their individual needs dictate. MyMetrica offers insight into threats and opportunities in real time, which then it claims can be addressed using ConsumerPulse, its consumer planning tool to target niche audiences. It offers a bespoke service for tracking podcasts, and uses the ConsumerPulse tool to build a picture of the audiences tuning in.

Nielsen BuzzMetrics

The Nielsen Company, based in New York and in Haarlem in the Netherlands, is a leading provider of marketing information, audience measurement and business media services. Nielsen operates in more than 100 countries. Nielsen BuzzMetrics is the company's measurement operation in the field of user-generated media. Nielsen BuzzMetrics works with companies like Canon, General Motors, Microsoft, Nokia, P&G and Toyota. The company operates a range of products under the BrandPulse name, tracking online word of mouth, buzz, issues and forthcoming trends.

BrandPulse and BrandPulse Insight measure user-generated content using proprietary data-mining technology. The products measure consumer attitudes to brands in real time and over a defined period. They quantify the volume of the conversations and their influence. The products measure specific issues, events and trends, and identify spheres of influence. Nielsen BuzzMetrics uses BrandPulse to measure other marketing activity including product launches, TV ads, sponsorship and interactive marketing.

BrandPulse answers about the volume, spread and influence of word-of-mouth practices and trusted consumer-to-consumer recommendations. It audits, tracks and assesses brand equity and is available in both written and online reporting formats. BrandPulse can provide e-mail alerts where fast responses are required. BrandPulse Insight reports focus on specific issues, insights or trends and can act as early-warning indicators. The reports cover a broad range of information, from hard numbers to subtle influences that affect brands or organizations. Nielsen also produces Brand Association Maps, which describe product attributes, messaging elements, competitive sets and related concepts and themes in a graphical format. It might indicate, for example, that third-party influencers that you involve have certain negative or positive associations that you were unaware of. Nielsen BuzzMetrics also produces BlogPulse, the freely available blog search and tracking tool mentioned earlier in the chapter.

Radian6

Radian6 is a Canadian company that began an early adopter program with a selection of PR and advertising agencies and their clients to understand the issues surrounding manual social media monitoring and analysis and to discover what does and doesn't work. Its approach is to work with agencies to develop bespoke tools. It developed a dashboard solution that allows topics to be quickly set up for monitoring, queries and analysis. Keywords could include names of brands, companies, products, competitors, issues or individuals. Once set up the system starts to track content immediately. It monitors blogs, top video-sharing and social networking sites, forums, opinion and review sites, micro-blogging sites, mainstream media and imaging sites. The dashboard has several user-friendly widgets to provide quick, easy access to specific bits of information. It shows where content is making an impact, which helps the PR person to understand what needs to be managed and where. The system uncovers the key online influencers by topic. The Radian6 system also allows for the easy export of data use in reports, presentations and spreadsheets.

SentimentMetrics

The SentimentMetrics team is made up of academics and marketing professionals. The offer is based around a web-based dashboard and a number of reports. The Buzz Report provides information on your daily, monthly or annual buzz. The Sentiment Report provides information on whether the coverage is negative or positive, the authority of the author and the source. The data is sortable and clickable so you can click through to the original article. The Stakeholders Report identifies people who are discussing your brand and provides a pie chart showing up to 100 of your main brand influencers. This chart is also clickable so that you can drill down to the original data. The Top Buzz Report provides information on the main themes of what is under discussion and the Mentions Report provides a lists of all mentions. You can combine and or exclude keywords. All of the tables and charts are printable and you can export the data tables to Excel. SentimentMetrics is available to trial free for a 14 day period.

TNS Media Intelligence

TNS Media Intelligence provides social web analysis or what it describes as market influence analytics through Cymfony. Its proprietary platform, Orchestra, integrates natural language processing (NLP) technology with human expert analysis to identify issues and trends impacting on its clients. Orchestra provides an online dashboard, which gives reports in real time, and Cymfony provides advisors who will assist in interpreting the findings. Companies can monitor coverage and track trends as they develop, which can provide useful market insight. Quantitative measurement provides data on specific issues demonstrating the direct impact of PR and marketing efforts.

Cymfony covers over 200,000 local, regional and international media outlets in over 30 countries. User/consumer-generated outlets covered include content from over 50 million blogs and tens of thousands of message boards, Usenet, consumer review and social network sites. Monthly reports are offered, highlighting key findings and trends. Individual campaigns and events can be monitored. Cymfony aims to determine the reach and influence of the top blogs and social media sites that impact on individual clients.

Visible Technologies

Visible Technologies was founded in 2003 and now has offices in New York, Seattle and Boston. The company employs a diverse group of over 70 professionals, with a combination of online technology and social media skills. In 2006, Visible Technologies formed a strategic partnership with WPP, one of the world's largest marketing communications businesses. The company has two social web analytic services: TruCast, which allows companies to track, analyse and participate in conversations, and TruView, which promotes companies' reputations online and raises their search rank. TruCast appears to be an industry standard solution that listens to what consumers are saying and fosters customer engagement by placing the messages in front of online audiences. TruView analyses search engine results, then promotes positive stories, sites and links, continuously optimizing results.

Vocus

Vocus is headquartered in the United States, with offices in North America, Europe and Asia. The company provides a web-based software suite to monitor and communicate online. The company has a proprietary information database of over 800,000 journalists, analysts and media outlets. Vocus was a pioneer in this sector with the first version of its software launched in 1999. The lastest version of Vocus, Summer '08, has built in social media tools. Each contact within Vocus with a Wikipedia entry links to that entry, giving access to useful background information.

Zeta Interactive

Zeta Interactive was formed in 2007 through an acquisition of Adverb Media, an interactive marketing, technology and services agency, by Zustek Corporation, an e-mail marketing business. Part of Adverb Media was RelevantNoise, a social web business intelligence tool. Like most of the competitor tools RelevantNoise monitors and mines blogs, message boards and online communities in real time. It tests effectiveness of marketing campaigns, gains consumer feedback, measures demand and spots consumer trends. Also, like many of its competitors it identifies critics and evangelists. Unlike most of the providers in this sector Zeta Interactive offers a 30-day free trial direct from its website.

Things to consider

There are numerous things to consider when you are selecting a partner to provide social media monitoring and evaluation. The information I've included on the providers above, has largely been taken from their websites, so it needs to be treated with the appropriate level of caution. This is an incredibly new sector and with some of the providers there may be a certain amount of smoke and mirrors and few if any will have a significant bank of experience. There are some questions that you may want to ask. First, do they do their own web crawling and searching or are they repackaging this aspect of the service? If it is the latter, then it is important to know where this information is coming from. If it is the former we need to know how effective this will be and how many pages of the internet they are indexing, or put another way, how much of the web they search. Social media is of its nature dynamic and is therefore much more difficult to index and search quickly.

Another major consideration is how you are going to share the output from your social web analysis with clients or stakeholders. If you can export data and images from dashboards this is a significant advantage. You may even want to provide your client with a dashboard, in which case you will probably want a service that can be white labelled. White label is software you can brand with your own company logo and house style. It can even be something that you could seamlessly integrate into a site that you can control so that the user experience is seamless.

14 Dodging bear traps

A constant theme of this book has been the transfer of control, from the few to the many, from the corporations to the masses. Any kind of marketing or public relations exercise in this environment is bound to face challenges and risks of backfiring. There are some principles that we should always hold close. Don't assume that everybody is of the same opinion on anything and don't patronize.

There is nothing we can do to free ourselves entirely from risk, although, by being aware, there are many things we can do to reduce the dangers. We need to try to understand the new threats that the social web has created.

Fact and fiction

We tend to believe that we have a natural instinct for the truth but we need to understand that not everything we read on the web is accurate. There is a safeguard here and it is called checking your facts. We can follow the old journalistic principle of getting at least two reliable sources for important pieces of information. Given the ease of search, we can extend this to multiple sources and ensure the veracity of the claim or story. False. Much of the internet is a mashup of other bits of the internet and that is a direct consequence of the ease with which users generate content. The resulting multiplicity of sources might suggest a breadth of knowledge but in reality if a factoid is convincing enough it can spread.

In fact, wikis are probably some of the most reliable sources of information on the internet, with Wikipedia being the most reliable of all. This is because the content is genuinely the result of multiple sources, sometimes hundreds of them. Even Wikipedia has been guilty of significant errors – often the result of malicious editing. Prominent US journalist, John Seigenthaler, was incorrectly named as a suspect in the assassinations of both President John F. Kennedy and his brother, Robert, for example. The false information was the work of a man called Brian Chase, who said he was trying to trick a colleague at work.

One common error is that of the false obituary. Because the death of a celebrated individual is of immediate news interest it is common for celebrities sometimes to receive obituaries from multiple websites arising from a single error. It has even been known for false obituaries to be published on separate occasions. Pre-written obituaries of entertainer Bob Hope were accidentally released on news websites on two occasions and Pope John Paul II was the recipient of three separate reports of his demise. Other widely duplicated falsehoods on the internet include a report that Barack Obama is a Muslim and that Bill Gates is giving away his fortune. This sort of widely distributed misconception is not the preserve of the internet. For example, the Great Wall of China is not, in fact, nor ever has been, visible from the moon, but the internet provides a distribution network that spreads these inaccuracies more widely and more quickly.

It is not just facts that are manipulated and distorted; the prevalence of powerful image manipulation tools means that photographs cannot necessarily be trusted either. Even the celebrated news agency Reuters came under fire for this when in 2006 it published doctored images of an Israeli air strike in Beirut.

We are in public

We need to treat our social networks and the conversations that we have in them as if they were conversations on a crowded train, very likely to be overheard, rather than hushed intimacies discussed in private. Whilst there are many places on the web where access to these conversations is restricted, all electronic communication can be forwarded and much of it is recorded in some form or other. It is far from uncommon for people to complain wistfully about their jobs from their Facebook Status, forgetting that colleagues, business associates or even their bosses are amongst their Facebook friends.

The English professional football club, Crystal Palace, dispensed with one of its players, 18-year-old Ashley Paul Robinson, after he announced on his Facebook page that he was about to have a trial with Fulham, a rival London club. The team manager, Neil Warnock, was very far from pleased when he was told of Ashley's Facebook boast and promptly released him from the club with the words: 'It's probably better that he looks elsewhere to further his career.'

Brandjacking

When websites first became available, companies had to deal with the issue of 'cyber squatting', where individuals with no connection to an organization nevertheless registered obvious names for corporate websites and then sold them back, often at exorbitant prices. This practice was eventually stamped out through legal channels and in some countries with the introduction of new laws.

More recently, companies have had to deal with 'brandjacking' where an individual or individuals hijack a company's identity and pose as representatives of that organization within social media environments. The very nature of these environments allows ordinary individuals the same access or even better access than corporate bodies. This can make it easy for a person borrowing a logo and a little information from the public domain to assume the identity of a genuine corporate representative. One example of this was the arrival of ExxonMobilCorp on Twitter. For a few days this was heralded as an attempt by the oil giant to engage with customers at a very personal level and to invite public debate about its business practices. The author of the post was called Janet and her profile carried the Exxon logo and a background of a wall of corporate images. Her biography contained the company slogan 'Taking on the world's toughest energy challenges'. Although the feeds were not malicious they were not from Exxon. Alan Jeffers, spokesperson for Exxon Mobil said that 'Janet' wasn't part of Exxon's public relations machinery and they no idea who she was: 'We're happy to provide our positions via our Web site and conversations with individuals and groups,' Jeffers said, but Exxon had no plans for any presence on Twitter. 'She is not an authorized person to speak on behalf of the company. There are several inaccuracies. We take great care in having authorized people speak on behalf of the company. We want to make sure anyone who is speaking for the company is doing so accurately.'

Parody

The broad availability of sophisticated cameras, video editing tools and powerful design applications combined with the ubiquitous ability to publish has led to an avalanche of parodies on the internet. The 'Slob Evolution' parody of the 'Dove Evolution' video (give them both a watch on YouTube) is so well done and so humorous that you might regard it more as a homage than a parody. Various films from Apple like the *A Closer Look at the iPhone* and the Mac vs PC films have fared less well, with a host of spoof copycats appearing on the internet. There is little we can do to avoid parody but there are some common sense strategies. If your messages or the way in which they are delivered come across as pompous or arrogant then they are much more likely to be parodied.

Economies with the truth

There are all sorts of examples of truth economy on the social web, from Wal-Marting across America to Sony's flogs (fake blogs), from astroturfing to sock puppetry (see Chapter 4). There are also broader corporate deceits, such as purporting to have an environmentally friendly agenda, when you are just spinning a piece of company policy. This is an activity known as greenwashing.

All of these economies and distortions seem to have one thing in common. They get found out. There are a lot of very clever people out there with a lot of very powerful tools at their disposal. When you place something on the internet you leave fingerprints and there are universally available tools, from Whois to Google Analytics, that can follow those digital trails. If you pretend to be someone you are not you will be unmasked and if you say something untrue it will be discovered.

Failing expectations

One of the definitions of a crisis in public relations terms is of a gap between expectation and experience. The bigger the gap, the bigger the issue. The social web has introduced a new dimension to crisis and issues management and that is velocity. There was a time when a customer complaint, even a severe one, would circulate through the customer service department for weeks or even months before the consumer became so frustrated that they took their complaint to a journalist. Even then there was no guarantee that their tale of woe would ever make it into print or broadcast. Now that barrier to publication has been torn down. Within minutes of putting the phone down to a difficult or unhelpful customer services representative, whilst still consumed by the burning white heat of anger and frustration, the consumer can be publishing their story. They can add photographic or video evidence and they can invite the comments or even detailed case histories from like-minded individuals who have had similar experiences with the same organization. It is clear to see why this poses a threat. There are many things that organizations can do to minimize the incidence and severity of this type of attack on their corporate reputation. Ultimately, the only truly effective response is to provide good products or services and well-managed customer service. This is the same as it has always been and companies that did not serve their customers well have always been found out eventually. The difference now is the sheer speed at which this can happen, as Dell found out when it sold Jeff Jarvis a substandard PC (see Chapter 2 for the full story).

Tone of voice

The social web converses in a very different tone of voice both from the prior incarnation of the internet and from most of the corporate world. It is very easy for organizations to fall into the trap of using the language of the corporate brochure, the annual report or even advertising, sales and marketing literature. The response to this is usually either antipathy, apathy or plain old-fashioned disinterest. The tone of voice you adopt should be suitable to the environment; ideally it should be conversational and engaging. Remember also that the social web is a place where information and ideas are exchanged and that if you want to talk you should also be prepared to listen.

15 The major players

I believe that one of the most significant aspects of the social web is the demolition of boundaries and therefore to include a list of websites, networks, communities and utilities seems somewhat counter to the spirit of a space that is constantly being moulded and adapted by its inhabitants.

Moreover, the actual boundaries between these sites and networks are movable and unclear. For example, videos from YouTube can be in lots of different places, embedded in a blog, placed on a Facebook wall or clickable from a link in Twitter.

I also believe that the best digital PR campaigns will create their own spaces on the internet, rather than relying solely on influencing or promoting the dissemination of ideas and information through these existing channels, although they may incorporate an interface with some of them. The rush to embrace digital public relations coincided with something of a Facebook frenzy and so an early call to action was the cry 'We must do something on Facebook.' Whilst it has a phenomenal number of users, it has an equally phenomenal number of pages and creating something unifying within this vast network is a genuine challenge. Absolutely key to the success of PR activity is to have a proper understanding of the media that you are targeting. Facebook describes itself as a social utility rather than the social network or indeed anything else. Bearing that in mind, the key to working within the Facebook environment is to provide something that is of genuine utility value to the communities that reside therein. If that is not a genuine option, no matter, because the social web offers a myriad of alternatives.

Video sharing

There are a huge number of video-sharing sites and platforms and there is one familiar to everybody, which is head and shoulders above the rest:

YouTube

The gold standard for sharing video on the internet. It's a simple proposition: you load your videos and watch videos loaded by others. The sheer volume of users and content means that the experience is far richer than the idea suggests. Broadcasters and TV producers upload content and you can use YouTube as a music jukebox (there is even a facility to create a playlist). Video-sharing sites can pose a threat to companies where consumers expose faults or relay bad customer experience. There is the now celebrated example of the 2004 video of the $50 heavy-duty Kryptonite bike lock being picked in seconds using a plastic ballpoint pen. YouTube can equally be a place where companies can promote themselves, providing the content is engaging or gives something back – for example, a 'how to' video for an electronic gadget would be valid – but YouTube is no place for your corporate video.

Social networks

Although social networking sites have been in existence since the mid-1990s they only really came to prominence a decade or so later. They vary in approach; some are built around business networking, others are purely social. Different networks appeal to different demographics usually based on age or geography. Skyrock, for example, is favoured in France and French-speaking nations, Orkut is popular in Brazil and India and Mixi is the market leader in Japan.

What the social networks allow you to do varies greatly but they are all built around groups of friends or contacts coalescing around each other. They can send messages, they can share music and video and sometimes play games with each other. There are common interest groups, a variety of utility platforms and applications.

Bebo

Bebo is a hugely popular in the United States, United Kingdom and Ireland, with in excess of 40 million users. It is one of the leading social networking 'brands', all of which offer similar facilities. Bebo profiles have five modules, including a comment section for messages and friends. Users can select from other modules to complete their profiles. Profiles may be personalized with their own background images. Profiles may include quizzes, voting sections, photo albums, blogs or list of groups that the user is a member of. Members can list their favourite music and include a video box with content from YouTube or from Bebo's servers or video content partners. The video aspect is an important development for Bebo. From November 2007, Bebo started to actively promote its open media platform for delivering audio, video and TV content to Bebo users. Media networks have their own specialized channel, which showcases their video content. Brands already signed up include CBS, Sky, Ustream. TV, BBC and Last.fm. Bebo offers three privacy levels: public, private and fully private. Bebo also allows users to make photographs private so only friends can see them. Some Bebo features are available on its mobile service.

Facebook

With 120 million users and growing, Facebook is the market leader in social networking. It was created at Harvard for students there but developed a global reach within three years. In late 2007 Microsoft announced it was taking a $240 million equity stake in Facebook, which suggested an overall valuation for Facebook of $15 billion. Facebook users can choose to join networks, based on their city, company they work for, school or region. The principal connection is with friends that you invite and whose profile pages you can access.

Facebook is much less customizable in terms of look and feel than Bebo or MySpace and doesn't allow users to have their own backgrounds, giving it a more consistent look and feel. The main features include the Wall, an open space for messages, pictures and video; Photos, where users can upload pictures or whole albums and can tag photos linking to the individuals in the picture; and Status, which allows users to update friends on what they are doing or what's on their mind in 160 characters or less. Facebook hosts more photographs than any other site on the web including Photobucket and Flickr, which, unlike Facebook, apply limits to the number of photos that a user is allowed to upload. The News Feed that appears on a user's homepage highlights updates like events, new friendships and birthdays. Facebook allows users to send virtual gifts to their friends, which then appear on the friend's profile. Facebook allows software developers to create applications that interact with Facebook features, which has led to the creation of a huge range of applications including chess and Scrabble (see Chapter 6).

MySpace

MySpace was the trailblazer for the current leading social networks. MySpace was launched in 2003 by eUniverse, a Los Angeles-based internet marketing company. MySpace and the company were bought together in 2005 for US$580 million by Rupert Murdoch's News Corporation, the owner of Fox Broadcasting.

Like the other social networks, a profile on MySpace has a number of features. There are two standard blurbs, About Me and Who I'd Like to Meet. The profile lists interests and details if you choose to enter them. The site allows users to alter the look and feel of their profile to a significant extent. Profile pages can be customized by entering HTML into many areas, allowing videos and flash animation to be used. Style sheets can be altered, changing fonts and colours, and background images can be added. MySpace offers a 'Profile Customizer' for those unfamiliar with HTML and CSS (Cascading Style Sheets).

MySpace allows images to be uploaded. MySpace's video service can be embedded, blogging is included and users' friends can leave comments for all other users to read on the main profile page. There is a bulletin board for friends to see and a groups feature, which allows groups to be created by anybody, either open or by approval, with their own page and bulletin board. The network also supports instant messaging.

The stand-out feature on MySpace is the way in which users can add music to their profile pages via MySpace Music. This has resulted in MySpace becoming an intrinsic part of the music business. The music is added to a player that is embedded directly into the profile page and can play automatically as the page loads. This allows unknown bands to post songs and use MySpace as the platform for launching their music career. There are profiles for musicians, which allow them to upload six MP3 songs. Unsigned artists can use MySpace to promote and even sell their music and established artists also use MySpace as an additional (to their own websites) space on the web to promote their music and interact with their fan base. It has become more common than not for artists to have a home on MySpace and music fans expect it. There is probably no other example as powerful where an established business has become so intrinsically linked with and reliant upon a part of the social web.

LinkedIn

LinkedIn is very much a business-orientated social network. More than 20 million individuals are on the network, including executives from all 500 of the Fortune 500 companies. The network allows signed-up users to maintain a contact list, with career histories of people they know and trust through business, college or through contacts already listed in your online or Outlook address books. The people in your list are called Connections. Users can invite non-users for whom they have an e-mail address to become a connection. By using LinkedIn you build up a network of direct connections, the connections of each of these become your second-degree connections and the connections of second-degree connections are your third-degree connections. These levels can be used to gain introductions through your contacts. Your contact databases can then be exploited to recruit or find jobs, discover business opportunities through recommendations or to research career histories of potential candidates so long as they are in your extended network. Those looking for employment might also look at the profiles of managers looking to hire and discover existing contacts who could introduce them. This limited access structure where contacts require a real pre-existing relationship, or a direct introduction is designed to build trust amongst users.

The network has a number of other features including LinkedIn Answers, which allows users to ask business-related questions for the community to answer. LinkedIn Groups allows users to create groups based around schools and colleges, industry expertise or individual professions.

In March 2008, LinkedIn extended its services to include listings for companies. Company Profiles combine LinkedIn network information with a company's description, industry statistics and some job listings. 'Company Profiles enable people to leverage intelligence from their LinkedIn network to learn more about companies; they will also serve as a vehicle for the companies to reach potential employees, customers, journalists and partners,' said David Hahn, Director of Product Management at LinkedIn. LinkedIn members can also access data on the typical career paths of people joining and leaving individual companies. They can also see how their current contacts connect them to employees at that company. Company profiles are based on the information from the 20 million profiles on LinkedIn as well as data from Capital IQ and *BusinessWeek* magazine.

LinkedIn company profiles might well emerge as a major influencing factor on the reputations of most companies and as such will be of great interest and importance to the PR profession. Other social networks include hi5, orkut and Habbo. There are numerous others, with many built round unifying interests or demographics.

Friendster

Friendster is a global online social network designed to help people maintain contact with friends and make new online friendships. The network has more than 75 million members worldwide. Friendster is a community that allows people to build their network through the friends they already have. Visitors create a personal profile, then invite friends to join. As they build their network they can view the profiles of the friends of friends. The Friendster's original intent was to facilitate online dating without the sleaze factor. It has become a major social network with significant growth potential.

Photo sharing

Photo sharing is the act of transferring digital photos online, and sharing them with others, either limited to a selection of people you know or making them publicly available. You can do this through dedicated websites and applications that allow the upload and display of photos. Photo sharing can also refer to photoblogs or individuals' online photo galleries.

Flickr

Flickr was launched in 2004 and three years later it claimed to hold in excess of 2 billion images. In 2005, Yahoo! acquired Flickr. In its early incarnations it was more about collecting and exchanging images found on the web rather than users' own pictures. As the site evolved it became more orientated to uploading and filing users' photographs, and new features were introduced to enhance this aspect of Flickr. This included the ability to tag images, marking favourites and the introduction of the Interestingness feature – where Flickr ranks images by identifying where the click-throughs are coming from, who comments on the images, how often they are marked as a favourite, the tags and other evolving mechanisms.

Bloggers use Flickr if they want to allow their readers to click through to a higher resolution version of the image on their blog. Users can create 'photostreams' or slide shows of a specific collection of images.

Photobucket

Photobucket is an image-hosting and photo-sharing website. It was founded in 2003 by Alex Welch and Darren Crystal and was acquired by Fox Interactive Media in 2007. Photobucket is used for personal photo albums and video storage. Users can keep their albums private, make them password-protected or make them openly available to the public. Photobucket has 20 million unique site visitors per month in the United States, and over 39 million worldwide.

Other photo-sharing services include Shutterfly, Kodak Gallery, Snapfish and Picasa.

Blogging platforms

Blogging platforms offer a range of services and applications based around specialized Content Management Systems (CMS) that have been designed specifically for creating and regularly updating blogs. These platforms allow you to manage and update a blog on your own server or through the internet via an interface in your browser that allows blog editors and publishers and authors to create and update content wherever they are. The main features are the same for most of them. They allow you to enter the key features of the blog: the headline, the body copy, the date and time the post was published (usually automatically). There will also be inclusions such as the comment system for feedback and discussion on blog entries. The systems allow you to tag entries to make them more searchable and they will all have a trackback or pingback facility that links back to other sites that link or refer to a particular blog entry.

You can enter text much in the same way as you would with a word processor but you also have access to the code, which allows for a high degree of manipulation of the look and feel of the blog if you have the skills.

Blogging is one of the most fundamentally important ways of generating original content on the web and therefore the ability to create and publish blogs should become one of the core skills of the digital PR practitioner.

WordPress

WordPress started in 2003 and has grown since then to be the largest self-hosted blogging platform in the world. It is used by millions of people every day. WordPress is an open source project, which means there are hundreds of people around the world working on its development and improvement. It also means that it is free to use. WordPress is customizable and can be used in a broad range of ways. WordPress.com is the web-based version, which lets you get started with a new blog in minutes, but is not as flexible as the WordPress you install yourself. In 2007 there were nearly 4 million downloads of WordPress.

Blogger

Blogger was started in San Francisco in 1999 by Pyra Labs. In the beginning there were just three members of the team funding the project through web design and build work. By 2002 the service had several hundred thousand users, and Pyra Labs was acquired by Google. Subsequently the Google Toolbar added a feature called 'BlogThis!'. This allows users with Blogger accounts to post links directly from the web browser to their blogs. Microsoft Office 2007 has built into it support for a variety of blogging systems, including Blogger.

Twitter

Twitter is the leading micro-blogging site, allowing users to write short blogs of a maximum 140 characters. The messages can be uploaded by a variety of means, via SMS texts or from a PC using Twitter or a variety of applications.

There is a considerable body of opinion that regards micro-blogging as being of considerable importance to the future of PR. Despite its very simple nature it allows us to do a vast number of things. We can build groups of influential followers who will read our postings, so in itself it is a direct form of communication. Within these groups of followers there is a disproportionately high number of journalists and bloggers who we can reach directly. The intimate nature of transmitting and receiving frequent micro-blogs creates a unique way of building relationships with other micro-bloggers, not least because you can direct messages to a single individual using the @ symbol in front of their Twitter name. Because Twitter is instant and if the journalists and bloggers are online and receive 'news', they can blog about it immediately — speed of publication being a highly valuable commodity when it comes to news.

We can also use Twitter as a very useful research tool. There are a huge number of applications built to work with Twitter. These applications can be used for research into what people are talking about here and now, and some of them represent these current conversations graphically with graphs and tag clouds, making it easy for us to share this information with clients and colleagues.

Content sharing

Digg

Digg launched in December 2004. It is a site where users can discover and share content. They submit links and then vote the stories that they link to up or down (Digg or Bury) and add comments. This creates a front page with the world's most 'dugg' stories. The original plan was to call the site 'Diggnation', but the creators decided on a simpler name. 'Diggnation' was eventually used as the title of Kevin Rose (a Digg founder) and Alex Albrecht's weekly podcast discussing popular stories from Digg.

Digg is clearly a very influential site and therefore so are the most active members of the Digg community. Lists of these members, who perform the function of self-appointed editors, are widely available.

Delicious

Delicious, which was known as del.icio.us up until August 2008, is a social bookmarking web service for storing, sharing and discovering web bookmarks. It is free to use and has more than 5 million users and contains bookmarks for over 150 million pages. Delicious has a 'hotlist' on its home page and 'popular' and 'recent' pages, a clear indication of current trends.

The site is simple to use and contains RSS feeds. All bookmarks posted to delicious are publicly viewable unless users choose to mark specific bookmarks as private. The public aspect is a particularly important facet of the site because it is focused on sharing and cataloguing sites via user-generated keywords rather than storing private bookmark collections.

Other communities

Last.fm

Although it is a social network of sorts, it is not of particular interest from a PR perspective unless you are working in the music industry. I have included Last.fm here largely because it is one of my favourite places on the social web. Last.fm is an internet radio and music community site. Using a system that it calls Audioscrobbler, Last.fm builds a detailed profile of your musical taste by recording details of all the songs you listen to either on the streamed radio stations it provides, on your computer or even through your iPod or MP3 player. This information is then used to create personal radio stations. Users can also create custom radio stations based on artists who are similar to each other.

16 The next big thing

The rise (and fall and rise again?) of Facebook

There was so much hype surrounding Facebook in early 2007 that sometimes it felt like Facebook was the social web. With its open applications and its ability to suck in other engaging content like Last.fm and YouTube, I began to envisage a time when it was the only place I would go on the internet and everything that I needed to do could be done from within. Its phenomenal rise in users appeared to completely support that proposition. Then, like a great many users, I started to lose interest in it. There were also numerous rumours of a fall-off in popularity, with users falling 5 per cent to 8.5 million in January from 8.9 million in December, according to data from Nielsen Online.

Then in the middle of 2008, Mark Zuckerberg, the network's founder, announced Facebook Connect, which would open up users' content details, extending its reach by allowing other websites to share content and services with Facebook. People will be able to log in to other sites using their Facebook accounts, and activities on those sites will be broadcast back to their Facebook friends. Perhaps the last big thing might also be the next.

Twitter – the early bird?

I believe that it is still very early days for Twitter. There was a stage in its development where frequent crashes would prompt angry bloggers to desert the service very publicly. But failings are rare and the investors have been piling in. Twitter's traffic has been increasing at a rapid rate, with a 500 per cent growth rate from 2007 to 2008. Its simplicity feels like one of its most powerful attributes. It is used very regularly by some of the most influential people in digital public relations like Todd Defren and Brian Solis. There are also powerful applications being built around Twitter that should continue to boost its popularity and range of uses.

Born again Friendster

'Don't count Friendster out yet,' said the *New York Times* in August 2008. The network has had a $20 million cash injection and a new Chief Executive, Richard Kimber, who joined from Google. Friendster is the top social network in Asia, with 33 million visitors a month from the region, more than double its nearest rival, and, until recent events, with the world's economic growth being driven from that region this must count for something. Friendster also has a portfolio of patents granted on social networking, so we should continue to see an expansion in its applications.

Huddle time

Huddle is a way to combine collaboration, online project management and document sharing using social networking principles. It provides workspaces for a variety of projects accessible online with no software to download and the basic set up is free. Huddle provides marketing and PR agencies with a customized extranet service. You can use Huddle as a secure area for your clients to transfer large files. Using

Huddle, you can reduce client approval times, collaborate between agency and client and reduce e-mail traffic. It avoids the need for FTP (File Transfer Protocol) servers and is a place to store press materials and track changes to press releases. It may not be the next big thing on the social web but it could become an important tool for the PR industry.

More mashups

Mashups are web applications that combine things from multiple sources and bring them together to form something that is greater than the sum of its parts. For example, the use of map data from Google Maps to add location information to any kind of location-based application. The term comes from music where samples are frequently used and songs might be mixed together to produce something new. The future of the social web is in mashups.

Imagine combining the huge volume of photographs that are placed on the web and tagged with detail about the individuals in the picture. Now, with sophisticated facial recognition software, we could be able to find out who somebody is and couple that with a great deal of data gleaned from social networks just from a photograph or image. Put that in a live situation and we could use a camera to inform us about an individual's personal history. Now mash all of that up with the network, closed circuit TV and surveillance cameras and add some mapping technology. Scary stuff.

Scour

There were two significant launches of new search engines in the summer of 2008. One launched with a blaze of publicity, which was immediately followed by a barrage of criticism. Cuil, pronounced 'cool', was launched as a new challenger to Google. The credentials were good: big money backing and a number of ex-Google staffers on the team. Despite, or perhaps because of the barrage of publicity, the launch was widely regarded as a flop. Why? Because the volume of coverage generated such a volume of traffic that the site couldn't cope. It ran slowly and some of the search results were surprising. I tried an acid test on launch day. I searched for 'Cuil' in Google. A news story on the launch appeared at number one and the site itself was at number two. I then searched for 'Cuil' in Cuil; no such luck. Towns and villages in Sligo, French cuisine, Lochaber town, scenic sights in Scotland and even some Gaelic results but no search engine came up. It was definitely lacking in 'Cuil'.

Have a look at the other search engine to launch around the same time. It is called Scour and launched with far less of a fanfare but it's interesting because it aggregates searches from other engines: Google, Yahoo! and MSN. It is also the first social media search engine because it allows users to rate searches, which should improve its functionality over time. I searched for 'Scour' in Cuil and it came in at number one! What's more, Scour actually pays registered users for every search it carries out. Now wouldn't you put your money on that?

Index

Accenture   87, 103
AdAge   22
Advertising   19, 83-84, 85, 104–05
aggregators   44–45
Agarwalla, Rajat and Jayant   60–64
Alexa   50, 88, 142
Allen, George   97–98
Alta Vista   53
American Marketing Association
   78
Anderson, Chris   28–29, 43
Andreeson, Marc   52
Apple   51, 95, 160
Arctic Monkeys   96
Aregbe, Farouk Olu   101
ARPANET   8, 50
Associated Press   140
Astley, Rick   119–20
astroturfing   35, 73, 89
Attentio   146–47
Auburn University   128
Audacity   46

Baghdad Blogger   26–27
Barker, Celia   63
BBC   13, 81, 87, 104, 140
BBC iPlayer   5
Bebo   2, 9, 10, 77–78, 165
Bell, Emily   77
Benn, Tony   20

Berners-Lee, Tim   9, 122–23
Birch, Michael and Xochi   2, 9
BlackBerry   59–60, 104
black hat   54, 118
blackplanet.com   101
Blair, Tony   70
blogger (platform)   26, 30, 171
blogs   26–36, 73, 170–72
   blogger engagement   27–30, 115
Blogpulse   139
Boyd, Stowe   38
brandjacking   159–60
brands   15–17, 105
Brin, Sergey   54, 79–82
Brito, Michael   106
broadcasting   20
Brown, Gordon   37
Bruce, Stuart   113–14
Burger, James M   62–63
Burkeman, Oliver   61
Buzzlogic   147
BuzzMonitor   144–45

Cadbury   120
Campbell, Alastair   70
Carter, Gary   7–8
CBS   12, 81
Central Office of Information (COI)
   3, 92
Chandlee, Blake   61, 63

Chartered Institute of Public
    Relations 68–69, 73
Cision 147–48
Classmates.com 50
Clifford, Max 67–68
Clinton, Hilary 98–101
Cluetrain Manifesto, The 75
CNN 99
Coca-Cola 15
Collective Intellect 148
compete.com 100, 144
Coren, Giles 14
Cunnigham, Howard G, 'Ward' 38
Crabhill, Julie 127
crisis management 86–89
cyber-balkanization 81

DAB 12
Daily Telegraph 81
Dann, Trevor 6
Darwin, Charles 105, 119
Dawkins, Richard 119
Defren, Todd 126–28
Delicious 49, 142–43, 172–73
Dell 17, 34, 106–07
Digg 9, 49, 143, 172
distributed conversations 116
Dougherty, Dale 1
Dove evolution 94, 119, 160
Dow Jones Factiva 148
Drudge Report 99

Edelman 29, 72–73, 127–28
Edwards, John 100
Electronic Arts 62–63
entertainment industry 102–04
Exxon 160

Facebook 2, 7, 9, 10, 25, 37, 50–52,
    57, 60–65, 94, 100–01, 108–09,
    159, 163, 165–66, 175
  Facebook Connect 65
Filter, The 81–82
Financial Times 126
Firefox 43
Five 78

Flickr 9, 16, 100, 108, 132, 169
folksonomy 49
Foremski, Tom 126–29
forums 24
Fremantle Media 7
French, Robert 128
Fresh & Easy 35–36
Friendfeed 116
Friends Reunited 50
Friendster 168–69, 176
Fry, Stephen 112

Gabriel, Peter 81
GM Europe 132
Google 10, 20–22, 26, 43, 52, 53–56,
    108, 117, 118, 132, 135
  Google alerts 88, 136
  Google analytics 88, 137–38
  Google trends 100, 136–37
Guardian, the 4–5, 14, 57, 77, 78,
    81, 140
Guerrero, Richard 106

Hasbro 60–65
Heuer, Chris 128–29
HTML 39, 84
Huddle 176–77

Icerocket 138–39
ID3 47
Internet Explorer 43
Iowa caucus 99–100
iPhone 104
iPlayer 77
iPod 5–6, 44, 51, 95
IPTV 11
Israel, Shel 57
iTunes 44, 77
ITV 13, 50

Jarvis, Jeff 17, 106–07
Jeep 108–09, 132
journalists 21, 28–30, 43–44, 67,
    101, 115, 125–32

Kate Modern 78

Kiss, Jemima   57
Kundhardt, Bronwyn   92

Last.fm   81, 172
Libsyn   47
LinkedIn   56, 57, 100, 167–68
linking   79, 117–18
logo 2.0   16
LonelyGirl15   126
Long, Doris   64
Long Tail, The   28–30, 78
L'Oreal   35
Lycos   53

McLaren, Malcolm   122
McLuhan, Marshall   82
Manchester Metropolitan
    University   111
Mann, Gavin   103
Market Sentinel   149
M*A*S*H   12
Mattel   61–63
Media Talk   4
Mellor, David   67–68
Meltwater News   135
memes   118–22
Merholz, Peter   26
Metrica   151
micro-blogging   36–38, 44, 140,
    171–72
Microsoft   51, 73, 92, 165
    Microsoft Live   53, 58
Millward Brown   57, 59, 150-151
Moore, Jo   70
Mosaic browser   12
Moss, Dr Daniel   111
Murray, Tony   111
MP3   25, 45–46, 96
MSNBC   99, 101
multi-channel marketing   103–04
Murdoch, Rupert   92–93
MySpace   2, 9, 50, 57, 96, 99,
    100–01, 108–09, 166

NASA   140
NBC   101

Neilsen Buzzmetrics   151–52
Netscape   52
New York Times   102, 106, 140
newspapers   4–5, 78
newsreaders   139–40
Nike   94–95
    Nike plus   95
Ning   52

O'Reilly Media   1
Obama, Barack   37, 98–102, 158
Osborne, George   20
Outlook   43

Pearson, Bob   34
Photobucket   169–70
podcasts   6–7, 44–47
Popular Mechanics   57–58
Page, Larry   54
Pax, Salam   26–27
Pew Research Center   99
politicians   67–68, 96–102
Prensky, Marc   93
Public Relations Society of
    America   68–69
punk rock   121–22

Quantcast   143–44

Radian6   152
radio   6–7, 44–45
Rather, Dan   96
Research In Motion (RIM)   59–60
Reuters   158
rickrolling   119–20
Roberts, Paul McHenry   31–33
Romney, Mitt   100
RSS   9, 42–44, 123, 129, 131, 139
Ruffini, Patrick   99–100
Rusbridger, Alan   4

Sabato, Larry   101
Safari   43
Sanger, Larry   39
Scour   58, 177–78
Schrage, Elliot   63

Scrabulous 60–65
search engine optimization
    (SEO) 53–58, 80
Second Life 57, 100
semantics 122–23
SentimentMetrics 153
Sex Pistols, The 122
Sheldrake, Philip 18, 86
Shift Communications 126–31
Sidarth, Shekar Ramanuja 98
Sky 5
Snakes on a Plane 122
sock puppetry 35
social bookmarking 48–49
Social Media Club 128–29
social media newsroom 130–32
social media release 56, 79, 125–32
Socialmedian 145
Socialmeter 143
social networking 50–52, 56
social search 57–58
Sofia's Diary 78
Solis, Brian 18, 129–30
Sony 73
Spinoza, Andy 70–71
Staniforth\ 61
Star Wars kid 119
Starbucks 107–08
Straw, Jack 2
Stride gum 120–21
[#]
TBWA\ 61, 83–84
Technorati 22, 117, 131, 138
television 5–6, 77–79, 103–104
Tesco 35–36
TGI 92, 150
Thompson, Charlotte 92
Thompson, Clive 56
TiVo 85
TNS Media Intelligence 153
TripAdvisor 15
Twitter 10, 30, 37–38, 44, 57, 100,
    106–07, 131, 140–41, 160,
    171–72, 176
  Twit(url)y 141

Twitterfeed 44, 131
Twitter Search 141

user generated content (UGC) 45,
    72, 73, 85, 102, 116
UPS 16, 135
Urchin 137
US election 2008 97–102
Uwins, Simon 35

Verrecchia, Alfred J 62
viral marketing 118–22
Visible Technologies 154
Vocus 154
vodcasts 48

Wales, Jimmy 39–40
Wal-Mart 72–73, 16
Washington Post 98
weblog 26
wherethehellismatt 120–21
Whitley, Shannon 128, 131
Wikimedia Commons 41
Wikipedia 9, 39–42, 114, 122, 158
wikis 38–42, 158
web 3.0 123
Weber Shandwick 29
Wells, Matt 5
Word of Mouth Marketing
    Association (WOMMA) 73
Wordpress 30, 170–71
Wordscraper 63–65
WPP 74

XML 43
Yahoo! 43, 53–54, 58
  Yahoo! News 99
Youtube 2, 7, 10, 87, 88, 96, 97–98,
    100–01, 108, 119–21, 132, 164

Zeta Interactive 154–155
Zonday, Tay 119
Zuckerberg, Mark 9, 51, 65, 83,
    175
Zyman, Sergio 85–86